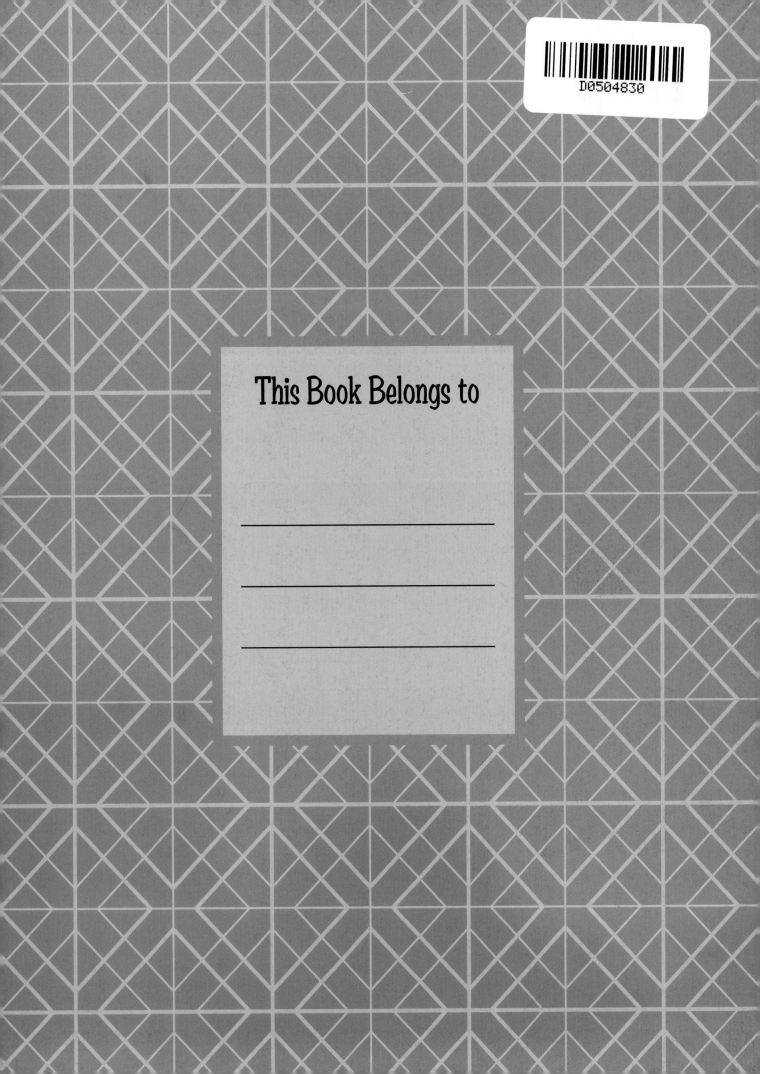

This Book Belongs to

_____

_____

_____

BART SIMPSON 2013 ANNUAL

For information address
Bongo Comics Group
P.O. Box 1963, Santa Monica, CA 90406-1963

Published in the UK by Titan Books, a division of Titan Publishing Group,
144 Southwark St., London SE1 0UP, under licence from Bongo Entertainment, Inc.

FIRST EDITION: AUGUST 2012

ISBN: 9781781164495

2 4 6 8 10 9 7 5 3 1

Publisher: Matt Groening
Creative Director: Nathan Kane
Managing Editor: Terry Delegeane
Director of Operations: Robert Zaugh
Art Director Special Projects: Serban Cristescu
Production Manager: Christopher Ungar
Assistant Art Director: Chia-Hsien Jason Ho
Staff Artist: Mike Rote
Lettering/Design: Karen Bates
Colors: Nathan Hamill, Art Villanueva
Administration: Ruth Waytz
Coordinator: Pete Benson
Editorial Assistant: Max Davison
Legal Guardian: Susan A. Grode

PRINTED IN ITALY

BART SIMPSON™
2013 ANNUAL

TITAN BOOKS

BART SIMPSON
in
BART vs. THE ONE-MAN SCHOOL

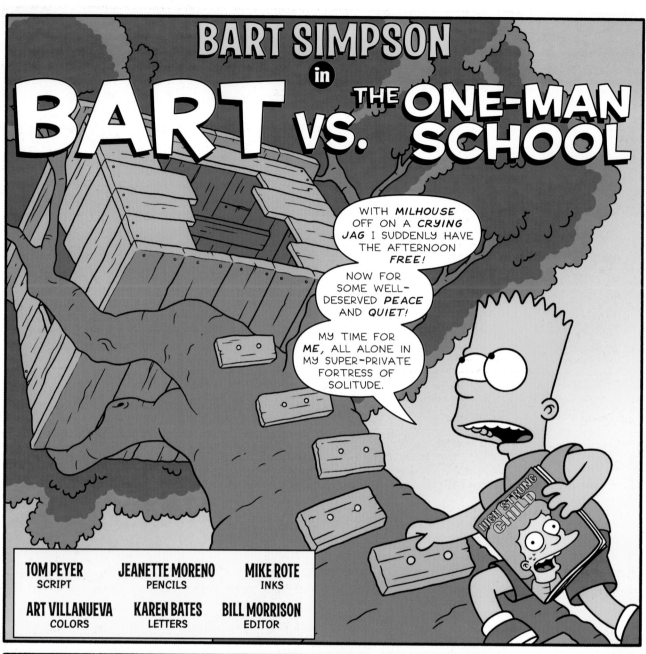

WITH *MILHOUSE* OFF ON A *CRYING JAG* I SUDDENLY HAVE THE AFTERNOON *FREE!*

NOW FOR SOME WELL-DESERVED *PEACE* AND *QUIET!*

MY TIME FOR *ME*, ALL ALONE IN MY SUPER-PRIVATE FORTRESS OF SOLITUDE.

TOM PEYER SCRIPT	**JEANETTE MORENO** PENCILS	**MIKE ROTE** INKS
ART VILLANUEVA COLORS	**KAREN BATES** LETTERS	**BILL MORRISON** EDITOR

AYE CARUMBA!

HELLO, BART.

SKINNER?

FORGIVE ME MY *TRESPASS...*

...BUT MOTHER *INSISTED* YOU WOULDN'T WANT TO BE SEEN IN *PUBLIC* WITH YOUR *PRINCIPAL!*

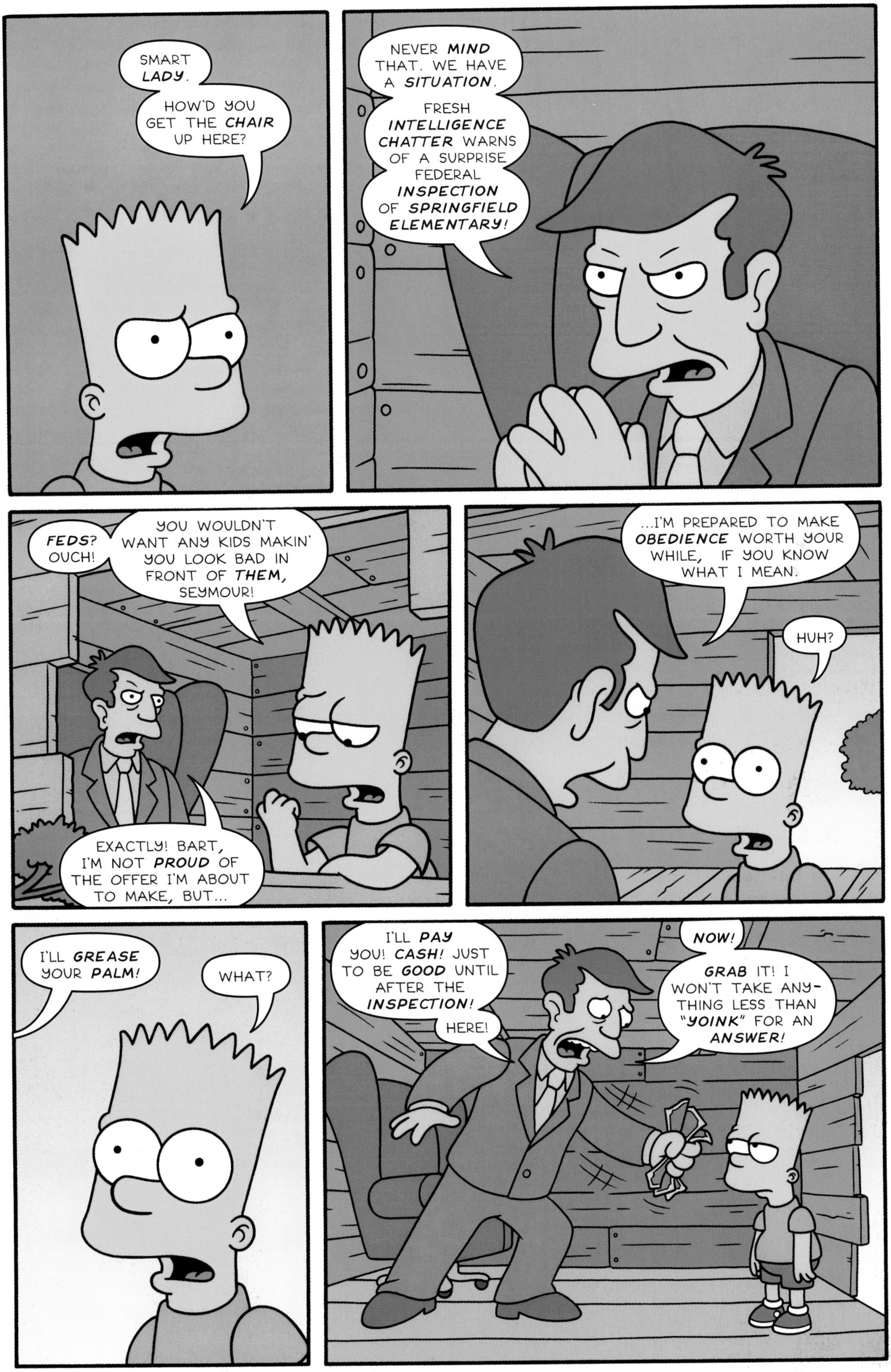
SMART LADY.
HOW'D YOU GET THE CHAIR UP HERE?
NEVER MIND THAT. WE HAVE A SITUATION.
FRESH INTELLIGENCE CHATTER WARNS OF A SURPRISE FEDERAL INSPECTION OF SPRINGFIELD ELEMENTARY!
FEDS? OUCH!
YOU WOULDN'T WANT ANY KIDS MAKIN' YOU LOOK BAD IN FRONT OF THEM, SEYMOUR!
EXACTLY! BART, I'M NOT PROUD OF THE OFFER I'M ABOUT TO MAKE, BUT...
...I'M PREPARED TO MAKE OBEDIENCE WORTH YOUR WHILE, IF YOU KNOW WHAT I MEAN.
HUH?
I'LL GREASE YOUR PALM!
WHAT?
I'LL PAY YOU! CASH! JUST TO BE GOOD UNTIL AFTER THE INSPECTION!
HERE!
NOW!
GRAB IT! I WON'T TAKE ANY-THING LESS THAN "YOINK" FOR AN ANSWER!

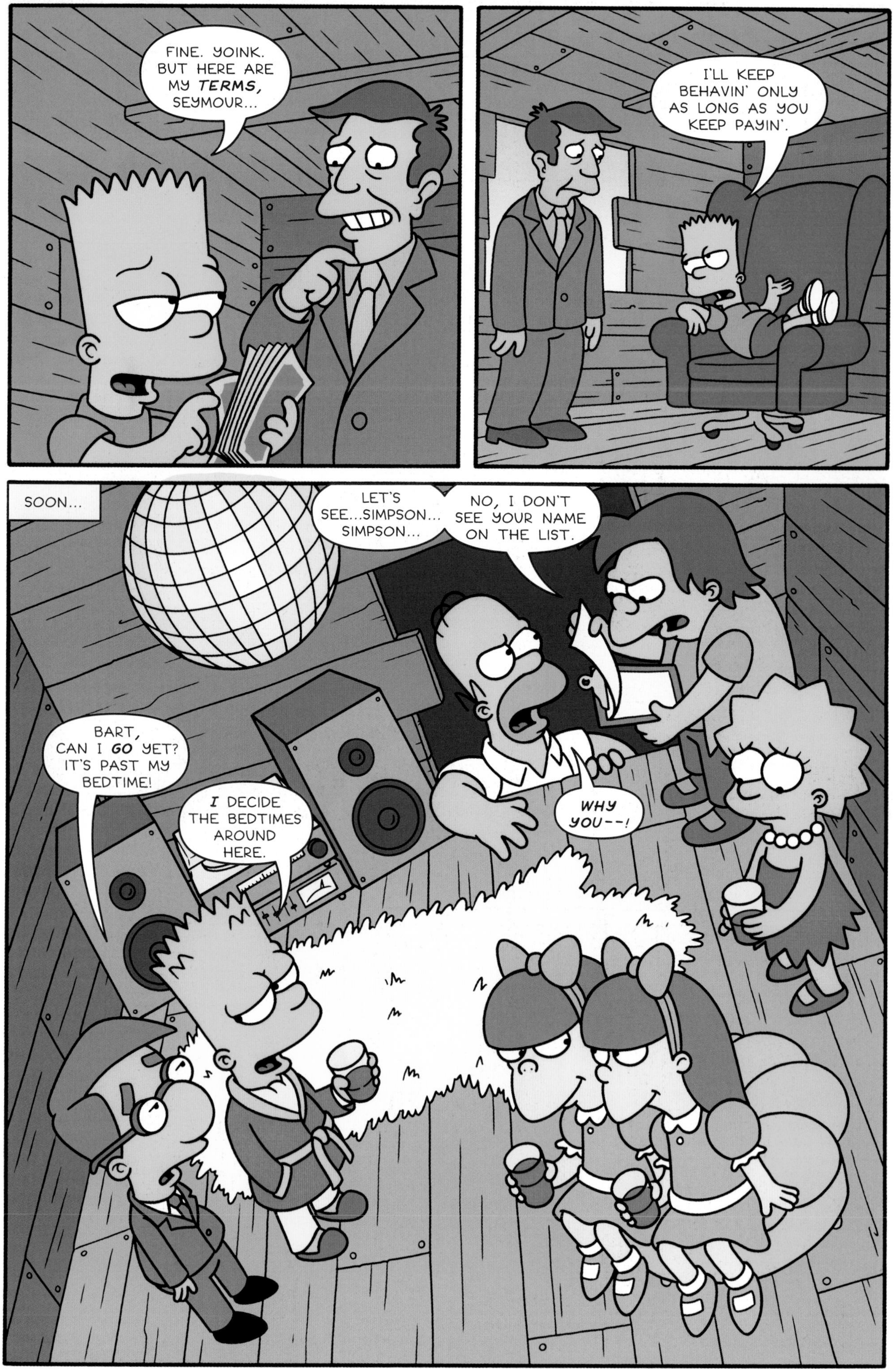
FINE. YOINK. BUT HERE ARE MY TERMS, SEYMOUR...
I'LL KEEP BEHAVIN' ONLY AS LONG AS YOU KEEP PAYIN'.
SOON...
LET'S SEE...SIMPSON... SIMPSON...
NO, I DON'T SEE YOUR NAME ON THE LIST.
WHY YOU--!
BART, CAN I GO YET? IT'S PAST MY BEDTIME!
I DECIDE THE BEDTIMES AROUND HERE.

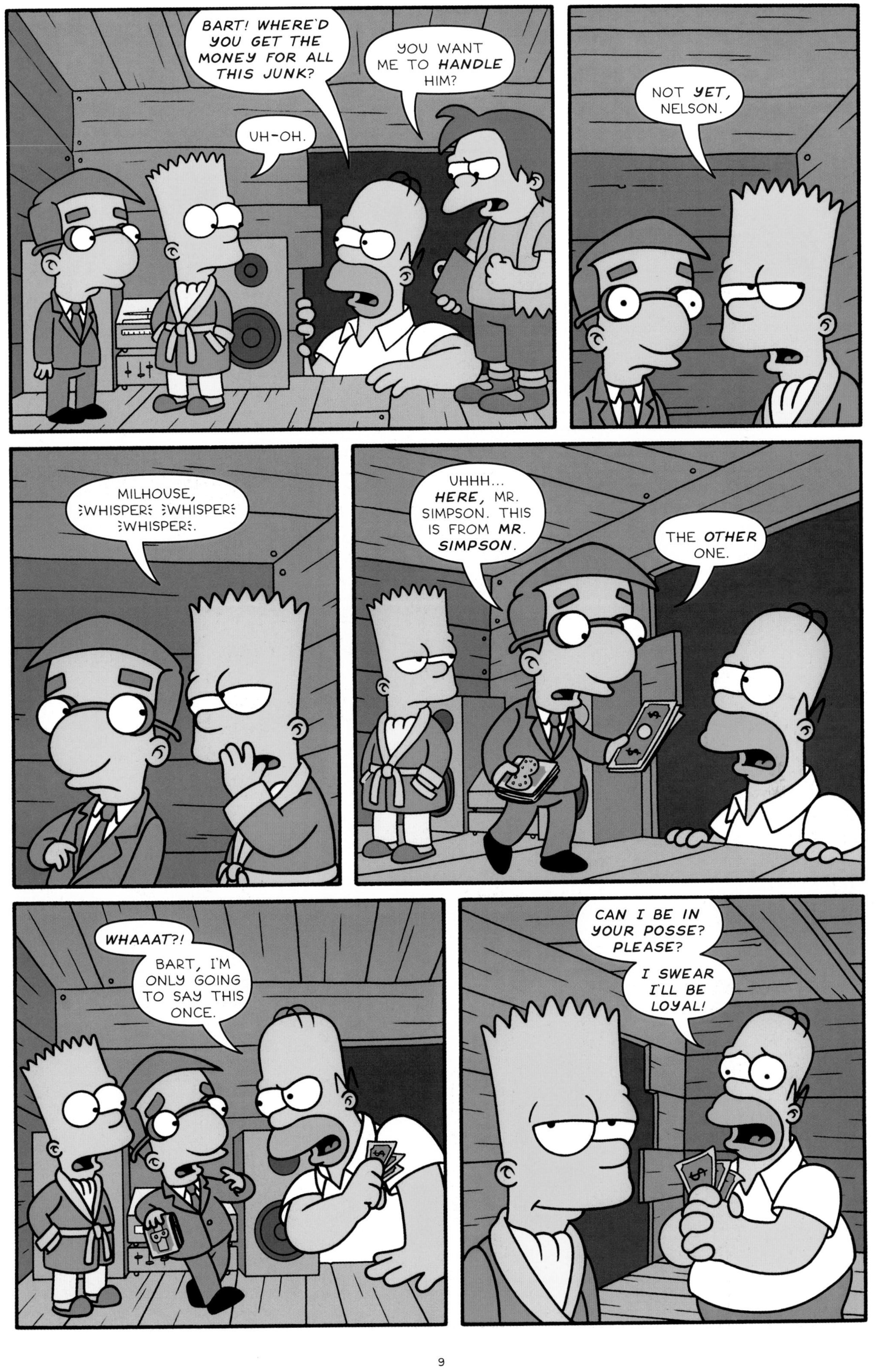
BART! WHERE'D YOU GET THE MONEY FOR ALL THIS JUNK?
YOU WANT ME TO HANDLE HIM?
UH-OH.
NOT YET, NELSON.
MILHOUSE, WHISPER WHISPER WHISPER.
UHHH... HERE, MR. SIMPSON. THIS IS FROM MR. SIMPSON.
THE OTHER ONE.
WHAAAT?!
BART, I'M ONLY GOING TO SAY THIS ONCE.
CAN I BE IN YOUR POSSE? PLEASE?
I SWEAR I'LL BE LOYAL!

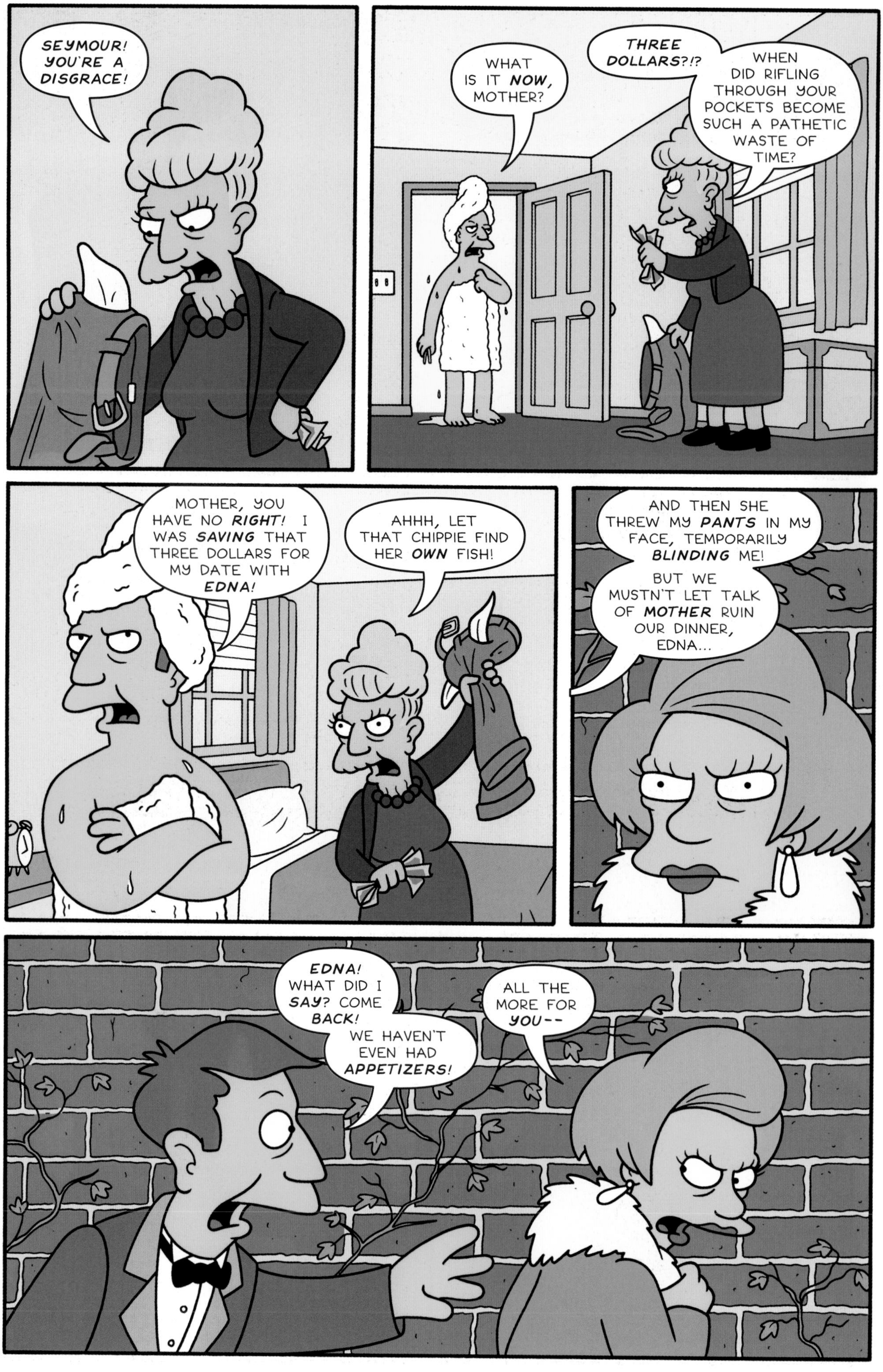
SEYMOUR! YOU'RE A DISGRACE!
WHAT IS IT NOW, MOTHER?
THREE DOLLARS?!?
WHEN DID RIFLING THROUGH YOUR POCKETS BECOME SUCH A PATHETIC WASTE OF TIME?
MOTHER, YOU HAVE NO RIGHT! I WAS SAVING THAT THREE DOLLARS FOR MY DATE WITH EDNA!
AHHH, LET THAT CHIPPIE FIND HER OWN FISH!
AND THEN SHE THREW MY PANTS IN MY FACE, TEMPORARILY BLINDING ME!
BUT WE MUSTN'T LET TALK OF MOTHER RUIN OUR DINNER, EDNA...
EDNA! WHAT DID I SAY? COME BACK!
WE HAVEN'T EVEN HAD APPETIZERS!
ALL THE MORE FOR YOU--

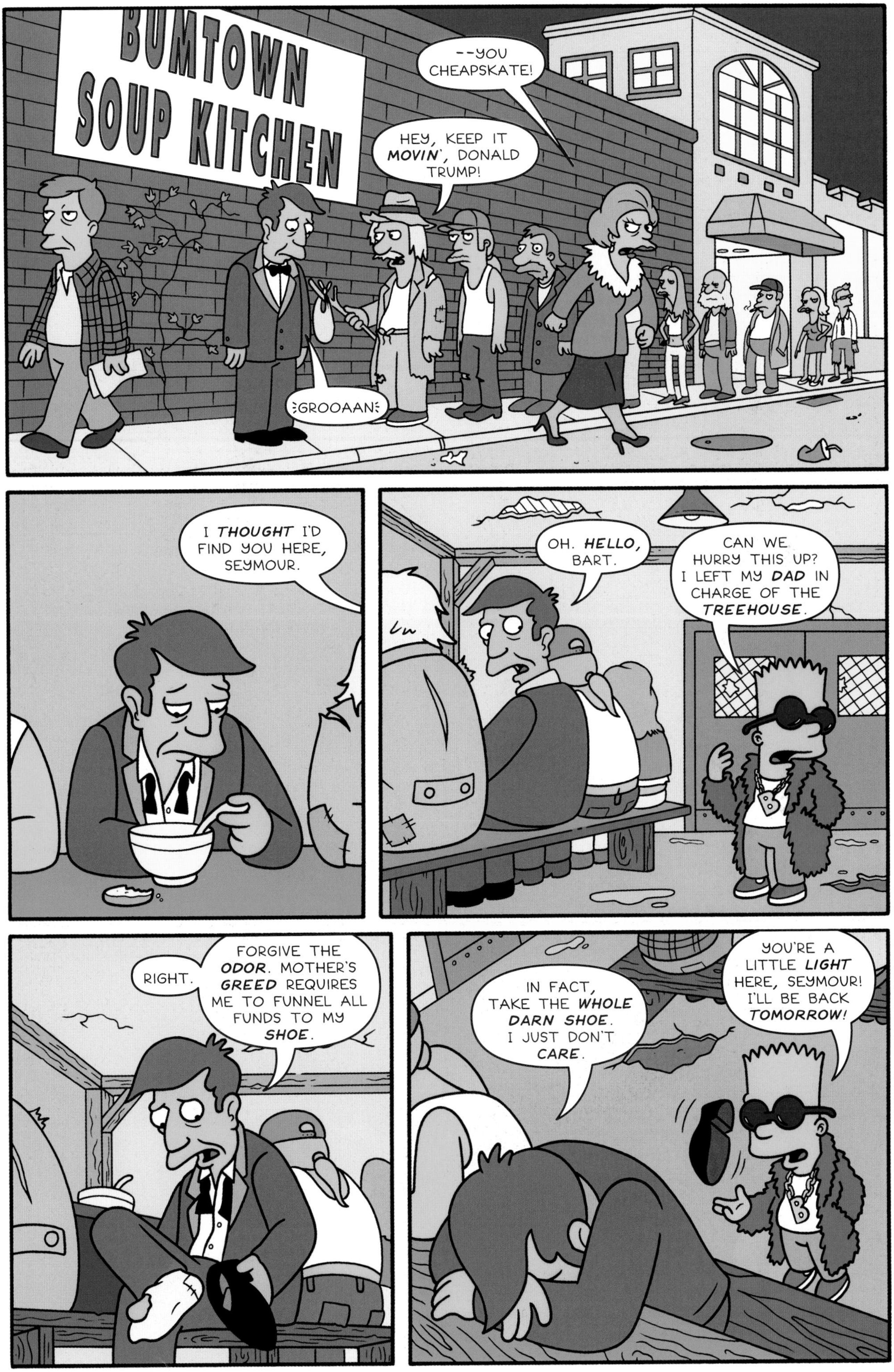
BUMTOWN SOUP KITCHEN
--YOU CHEAPSKATE!
HEY, KEEP IT MOVIN', DONALD TRUMP!
GROOAAN
I THOUGHT I'D FIND YOU HERE, SEYMOUR.
OH. HELLO, BART.
CAN WE HURRY THIS UP? I LEFT MY DAD IN CHARGE OF THE TREEHOUSE.
RIGHT.
FORGIVE THE ODOR. MOTHER'S GREED REQUIRES ME TO FUNNEL ALL FUNDS TO MY SHOE.
YOU'RE A LITTLE LIGHT HERE, SEYMOUR! I'LL BE BACK TOMORROW!
IN FACT, TAKE THE WHOLE DARN SHOE. I JUST DON'T CARE.

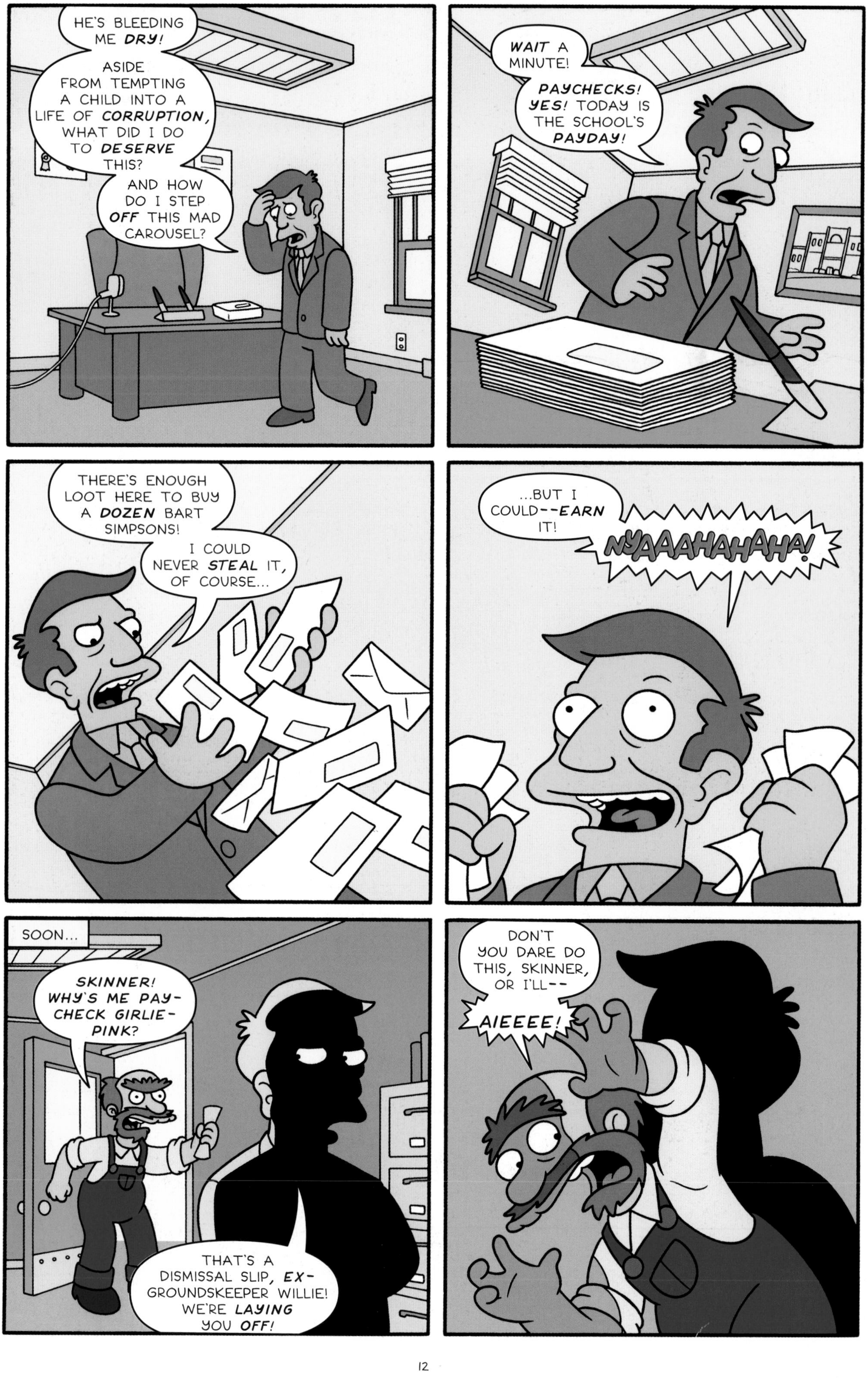
HE'S BLEEDING ME DRY!
ASIDE FROM TEMPTING A CHILD INTO A LIFE OF CORRUPTION, WHAT DID I DO TO DESERVE THIS?
AND HOW DO I STEP OFF THIS MAD CAROUSEL?
WAIT A MINUTE!
PAYCHECKS! YES! TODAY IS THE SCHOOL'S PAYDAY!
THERE'S ENOUGH LOOT HERE TO BUY A DOZEN BART SIMPSONS!
I COULD NEVER STEAL IT, OF COURSE...
...BUT I COULD--EARN IT!
NYAAAHAHAHA!
SOON...
SKINNER! WHY'S ME PAY-CHECK GIRLIE-PINK?
THAT'S A DISMISSAL SLIP, EX-GROUNDSKEEPER WILLIE! WE'RE LAYING YOU OFF!
DON'T YOU DARE DO THIS, SKINNER, OR I'LL--
AIEEEE!

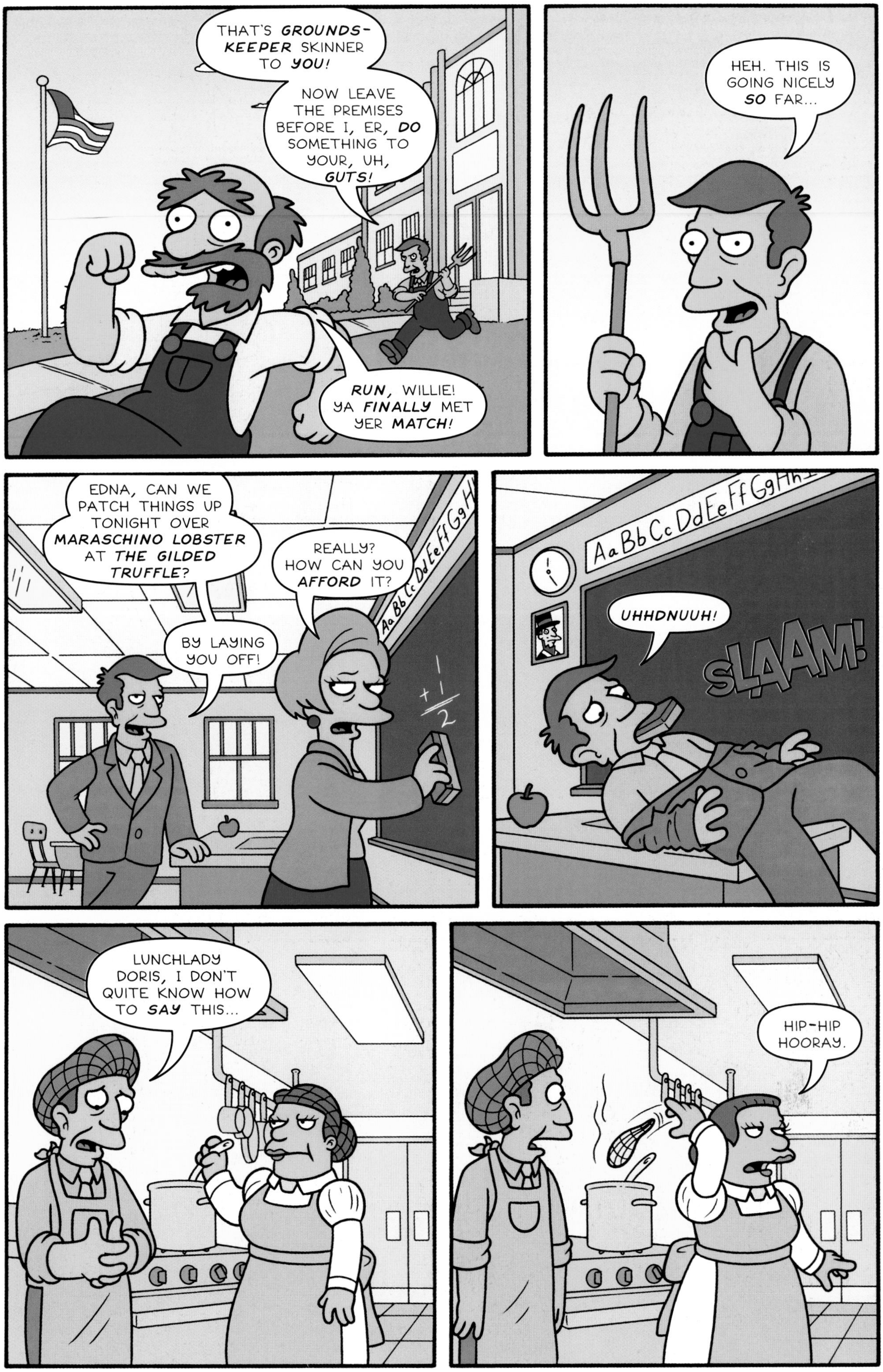
THAT'S GROUNDS-KEEPER SKINNER TO YOU!
NOW LEAVE THE PREMISES BEFORE I, ER, DO SOMETHING TO YOUR, UH, GUTS!
RUN, WILLIE! YA FINALLY MET YER MATCH!
HEH. THIS IS GOING NICELY SO FAR...
EDNA, CAN WE PATCH THINGS UP TONIGHT OVER MARASCHINO LOBSTER AT THE GILDED TRUFFLE?
REALLY? HOW CAN YOU AFFORD IT?
BY LAYING YOU OFF!
UHHDNUUH!
SLAAM!
LUNCHLADY DORIS, I DON'T QUITE KNOW HOW TO SAY THIS...
HIP-HIP HOORAY.

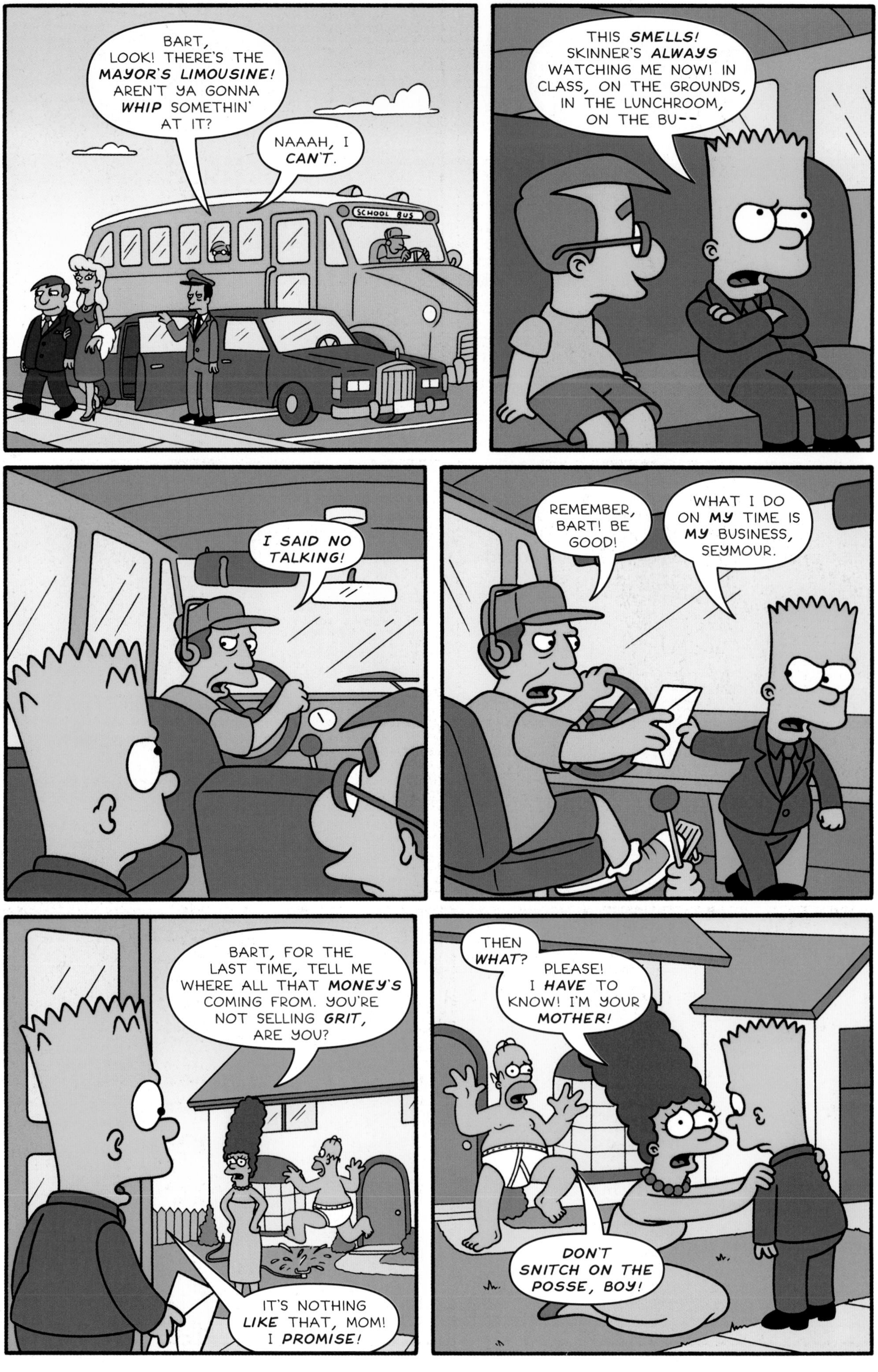
BART, LOOK! THERE'S THE MAYOR'S LIMOUSINE! AREN'T YA GONNA WHIP SOMETHIN' AT IT?
NAAAH, I CAN'T.
SCHOOL BUS
THIS SMELLS! SKINNER'S ALWAYS WATCHING ME NOW! IN CLASS, ON THE GROUNDS, IN THE LUNCHROOM, ON THE BU--
I SAID NO TALKING!
REMEMBER, BART! BE GOOD!
WHAT I DO ON MY TIME IS MY BUSINESS, SEYMOUR.
BART, FOR THE LAST TIME, TELL ME WHERE ALL THAT MONEY'S COMING FROM. YOU'RE NOT SELLING GRIT, ARE YOU?
IT'S NOTHING LIKE THAT, MOM! I PROMISE!
THEN WHAT?
PLEASE! I HAVE TO KNOW! I'M YOUR MOTHER!
DON'T SNITCH ON THE POSSE, BOY!

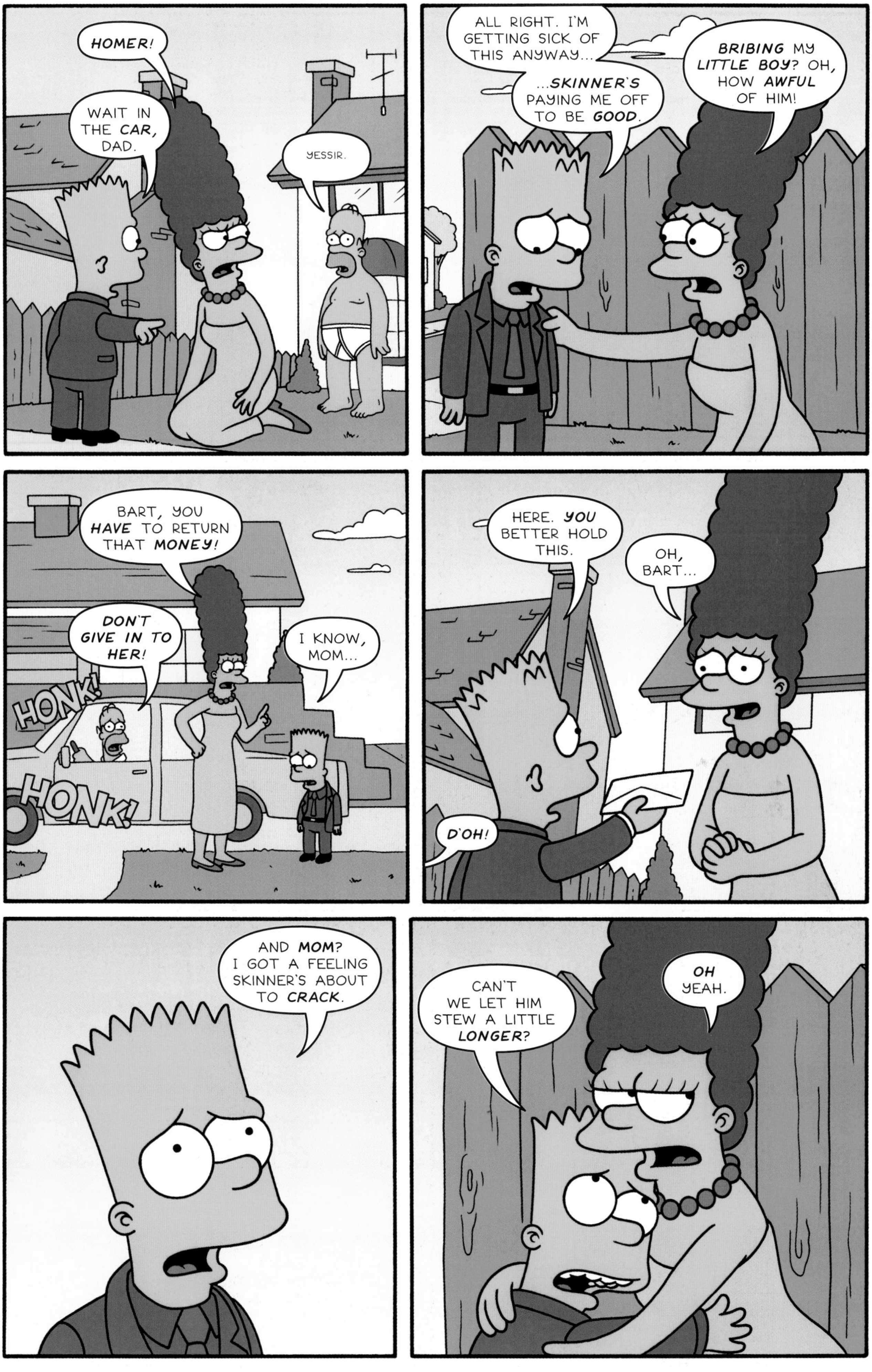
HOMER!
WAIT IN THE CAR, DAD.
YESSIR.
ALL RIGHT. I'M GETTING SICK OF THIS ANYWAY...
...SKINNER'S PAYING ME OFF TO BE GOOD.
BRIBING MY LITTLE BOY? OH, HOW AWFUL OF HIM!
BART, YOU HAVE TO RETURN THAT MONEY!
DON'T GIVE IN TO HER!
I KNOW, MOM...
HONK!
HONK!
HERE. YOU BETTER HOLD THIS.
OH, BART...
D'OH!
AND MOM? I GOT A FEELING SKINNER'S ABOUT TO CRACK.
CAN'T WE LET HIM STEW A LITTLE LONGER?
OH YEAH.

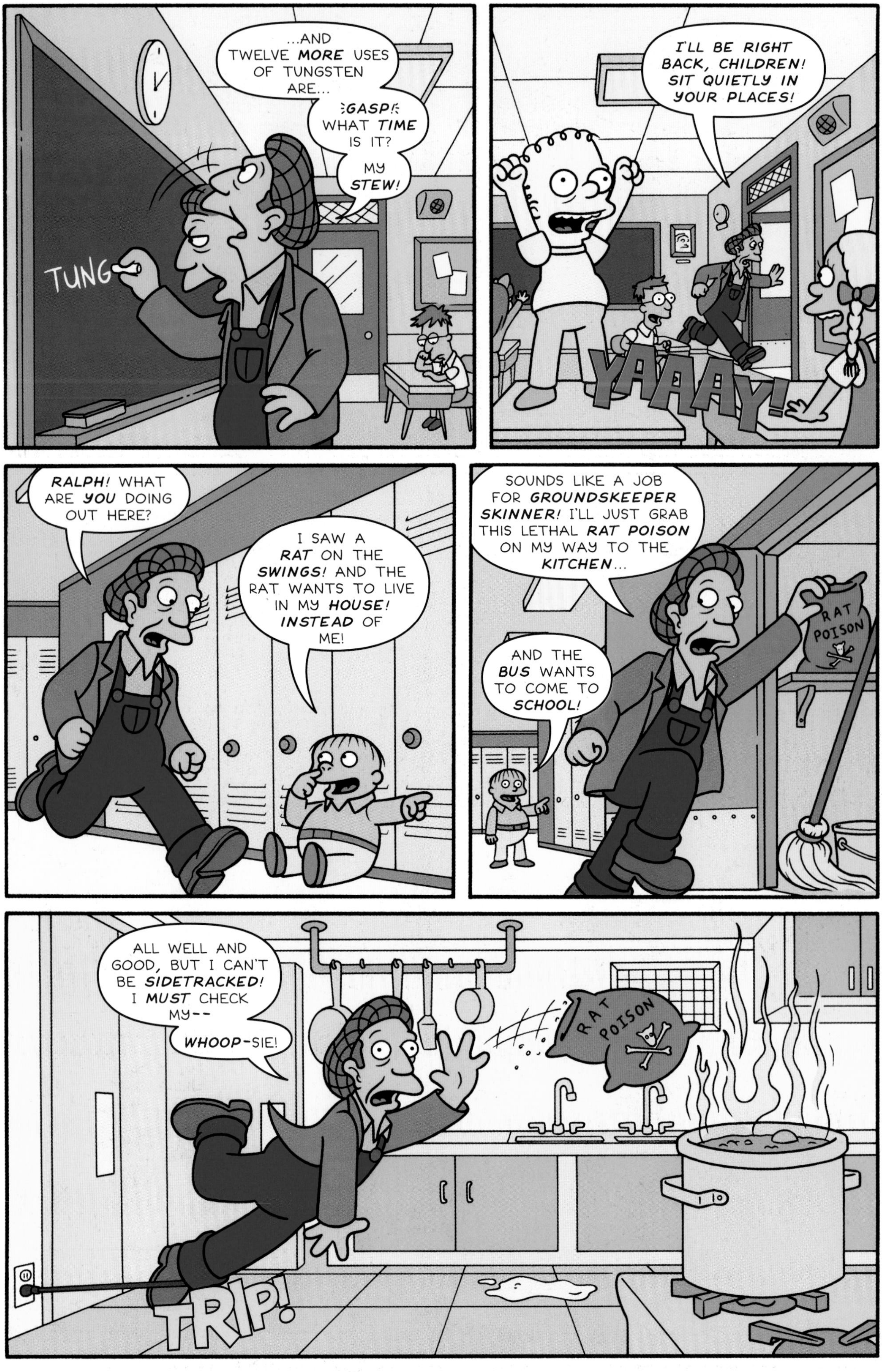

...AND TWELVE MORE USES OF TUNGSTEN ARE...
TUNG
⁝GASP!⁝ WHAT TIME IS IT?
MY STEW!
I'LL BE RIGHT BACK, CHILDREN! SIT QUIETLY IN YOUR PLACES!
YAAAY!
RALPH! WHAT ARE YOU DOING OUT HERE?
I SAW A RAT ON THE SWINGS! AND THE RAT WANTS TO LIVE IN MY HOUSE! INSTEAD OF ME!
SOUNDS LIKE A JOB FOR GROUNDSKEEPER SKINNER! I'LL JUST GRAB THIS LETHAL RAT POISON ON MY WAY TO THE KITCHEN...
RAT POISON
AND THE BUS WANTS TO COME TO SCHOOL!
ALL WELL AND GOOD, BUT I CAN'T BE SIDETRACKED! I MUST CHECK MY--
WHOOP-SIE!
RAT POISON
TRIP!

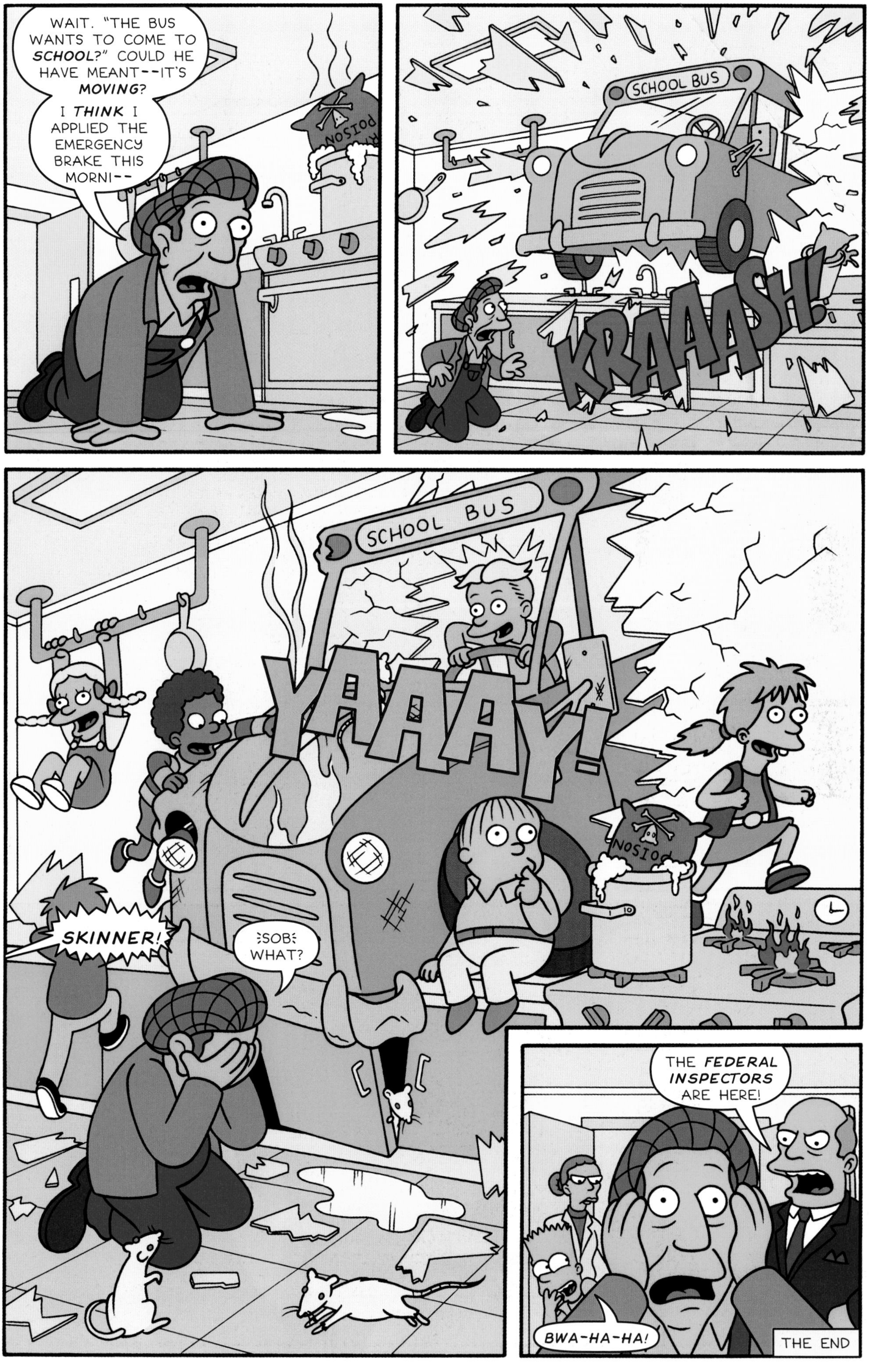
WAIT. "THE BUS WANTS TO COME TO SCHOOL?" COULD HE HAVE MEANT--IT'S MOVING?
I THINK I APPLIED THE EMERGENCY BRAKE THIS MORNI--
POISON
SCHOOL BUS
KRAAASH!
SCHOOL BUS
YAAAY!
POISON
SKINNER!
SOB WHAT?
THE FEDERAL INSPECTORS ARE HERE!
BWA-HA-HA!
THE END

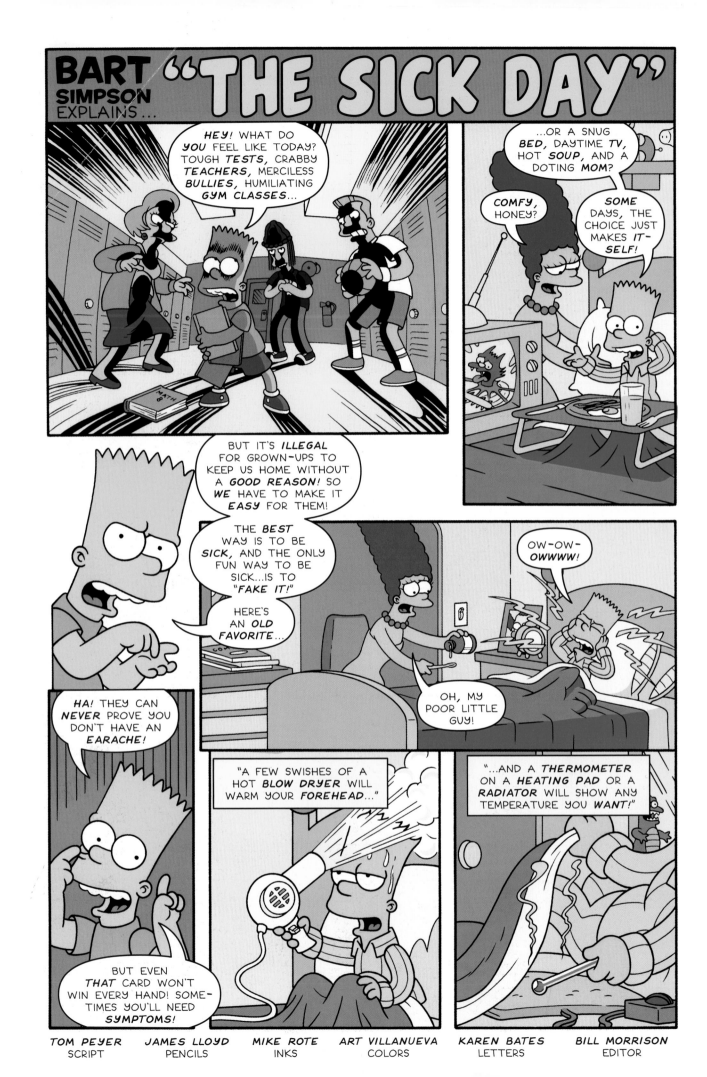

BART SIMPSON EXPLAINS... "THE SICK DAY"

HEY! WHAT DO *YOU* FEEL LIKE TODAY? TOUGH *TESTS*, CRABBY *TEACHERS*, MERCILESS *BULLIES*, HUMILIATING *GYM CLASSES*...

...OR A SNUG *BED*, DAYTIME *TV*, HOT *SOUP*, AND A DOTING *MOM*?

COMFY, HONEY?

SOME DAYS, THE CHOICE JUST MAKES *IT-SELF!*

BUT IT'S *ILLEGAL* FOR GROWN-UPS TO KEEP US HOME WITHOUT A *GOOD REASON!* SO *WE* HAVE TO MAKE IT *EASY* FOR THEM!

THE *BEST* WAY IS TO BE *SICK*, AND THE ONLY FUN WAY TO BE SICK...IS TO "*FAKE IT!*"

HERE'S AN *OLD* FAVORITE...

OW-OW-OWWWW!

OH, MY POOR LITTLE GUY!

HA! THEY CAN *NEVER* PROVE YOU DON'T HAVE AN *EARACHE!*

"A FEW SWISHES OF A HOT *BLOW DRYER* WILL WARM YOUR *FOREHEAD*..."

"...AND A *THERMOMETER* ON A *HEATING PAD* OR A *RADIATOR* WILL SHOW ANY TEMPERATURE YOU *WANT!*"

BUT EVEN *THAT* CARD WON'T WIN EVERY HAND! SOME-TIMES YOU'LL NEED *SYMPTOMS!*

TOM PEYER
SCRIPT

JAMES LLOYD
PENCILS

MIKE ROTE
INKS

ART VILLANUEVA
COLORS

KAREN BATES
LETTERS

BILL MORRISON
EDITOR

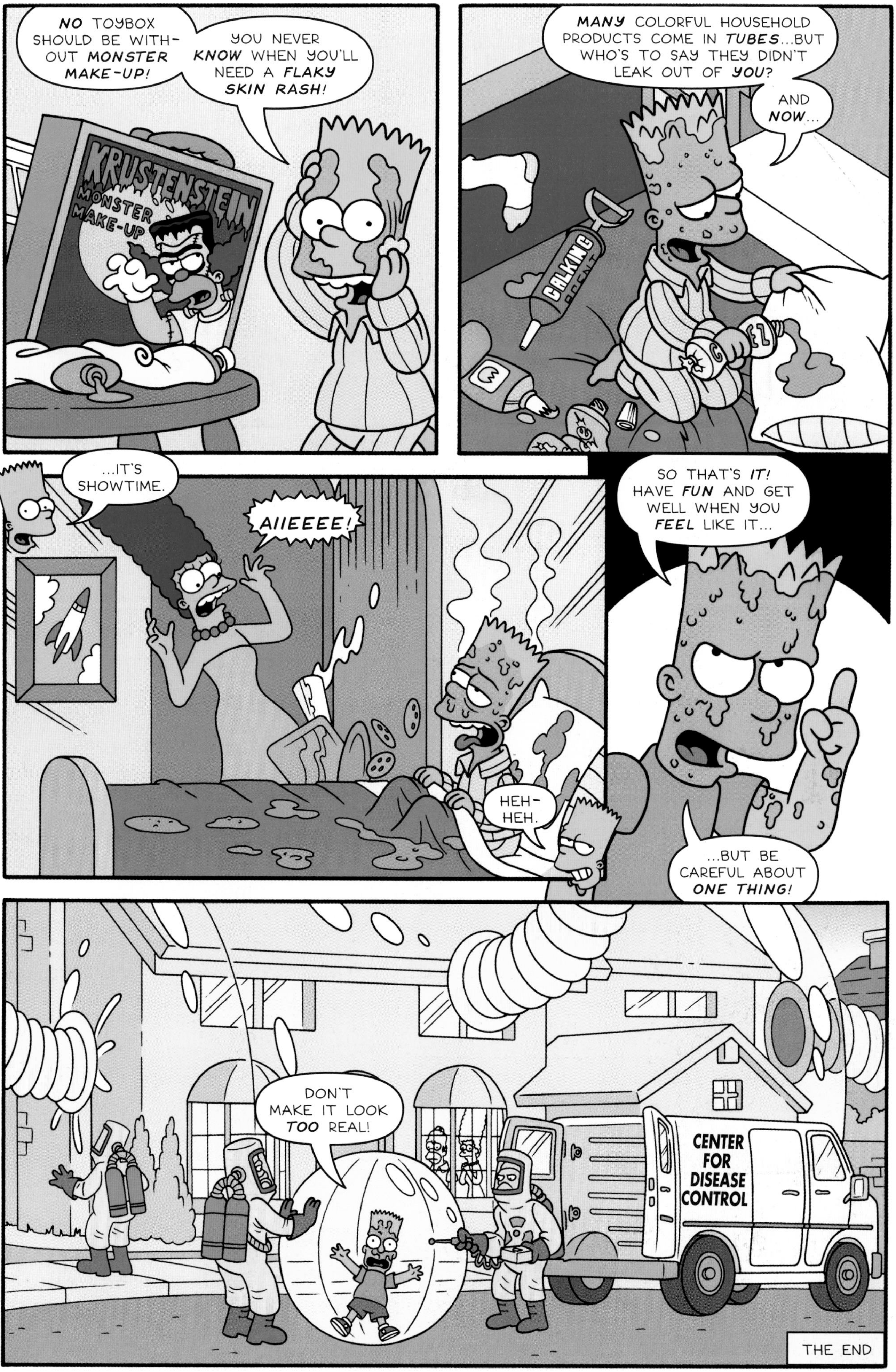
NO TOYBOX SHOULD BE WITH-OUT MONSTER MAKE-UP!
YOU NEVER KNOW WHEN YOU'LL NEED A FLAKY SKIN RASH!
KRUSTENSTEIN MONSTER MAKE-UP
MANY COLORFUL HOUSEHOLD PRODUCTS COME IN TUBES...BUT WHO'S TO SAY THEY DIDN'T LEAK OUT OF YOU?
AND NOW...
CALKING
...IT'S SHOWTIME.
AIIEEEE!
HEH-HEH.
SO THAT'S IT! HAVE FUN AND GET WELL WHEN YOU FEEL LIKE IT...
...BUT BE CAREFUL ABOUT ONE THING!
DON'T MAKE IT LOOK TOO REAL!
CENTER FOR DISEASE CONTROL
THE END

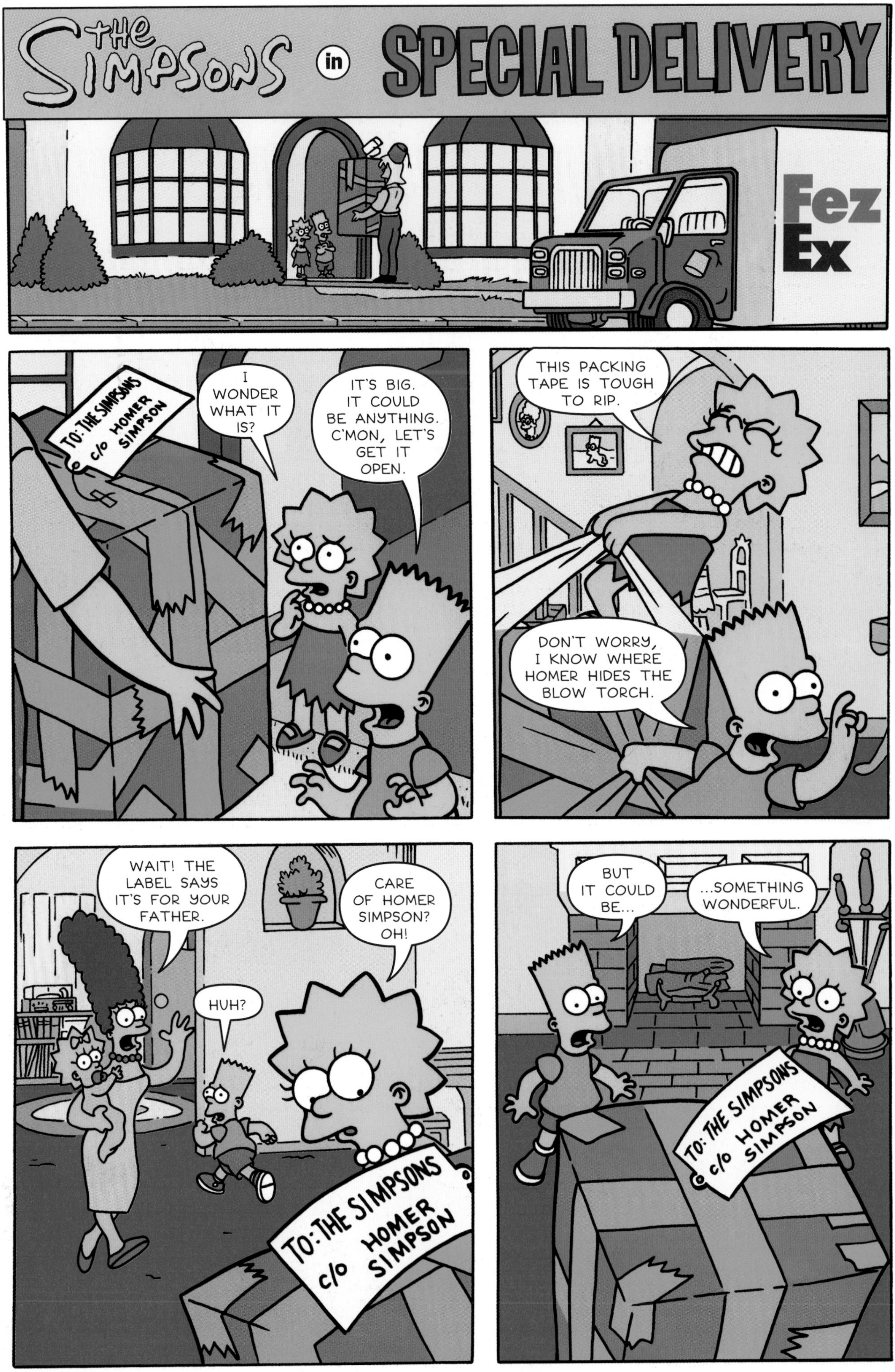
THE SIMPSONS in SPECIAL DELIVERY
Fez Ex
TO: THE SIMPSONS c/o HOMER SIMPSON
I WONDER WHAT IT IS?
IT'S BIG. IT COULD BE ANYTHING. C'MON, LET'S GET IT OPEN.
THIS PACKING TAPE IS TOUGH TO RIP.
DON'T WORRY, I KNOW WHERE HOMER HIDES THE BLOW TORCH.
WAIT! THE LABEL SAYS IT'S FOR YOUR FATHER.
CARE OF HOMER SIMPSON? OH!
HUH?
TO: THE SIMPSONS c/o HOMER SIMPSON
BUT IT COULD BE...
...SOMETHING WONDERFUL.
TO: THE SIMPSONS c/o HOMER SIMPSON

JAMES BATES	*JOHN DELANEY*	*HOWARD SHUM*	*ART VILLANUEVA*	*KAREN BATES*	*BILL MORRISON*
SCRIPT	PENCILS	INKS	COLORS	LETTERS	EDITOR

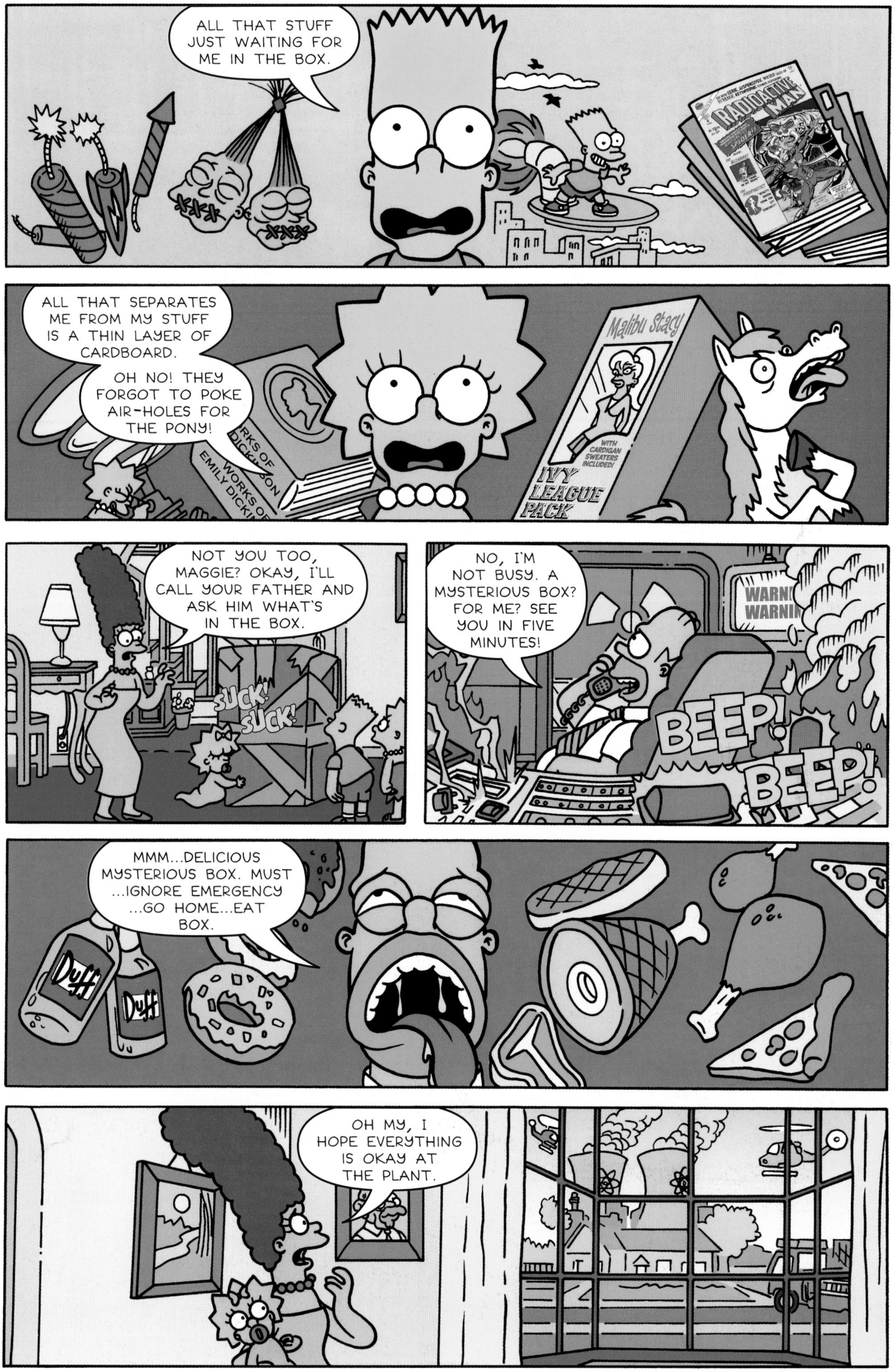
ALL THAT STUFF JUST WAITING FOR ME IN THE BOX.
RADIOACTIVE MAN
ALL THAT SEPARATES ME FROM MY STUFF IS A THIN LAYER OF CARDBOARD.
OH NO! THEY FORGOT TO POKE AIR-HOLES FOR THE PONY!
Malibu Stacy
WITH CARDIGAN SWEATERS INCLUDED!
IVY LEAGUE PACK
NOT YOU TOO, MAGGIE? OKAY, I'LL CALL YOUR FATHER AND ASK HIM WHAT'S IN THE BOX.
SUCK! SUCK!
NO, I'M NOT BUSY. A MYSTERIOUS BOX? FOR ME? SEE YOU IN FIVE MINUTES!
BEEP! BEEP!
MMM...DELICIOUS MYSTERIOUS BOX. MUST ...IGNORE EMERGENCY ...GO HOME...EAT BOX.
Duff
Duff
OH MY, I HOPE EVERYTHING IS OKAY AT THE PLANT.

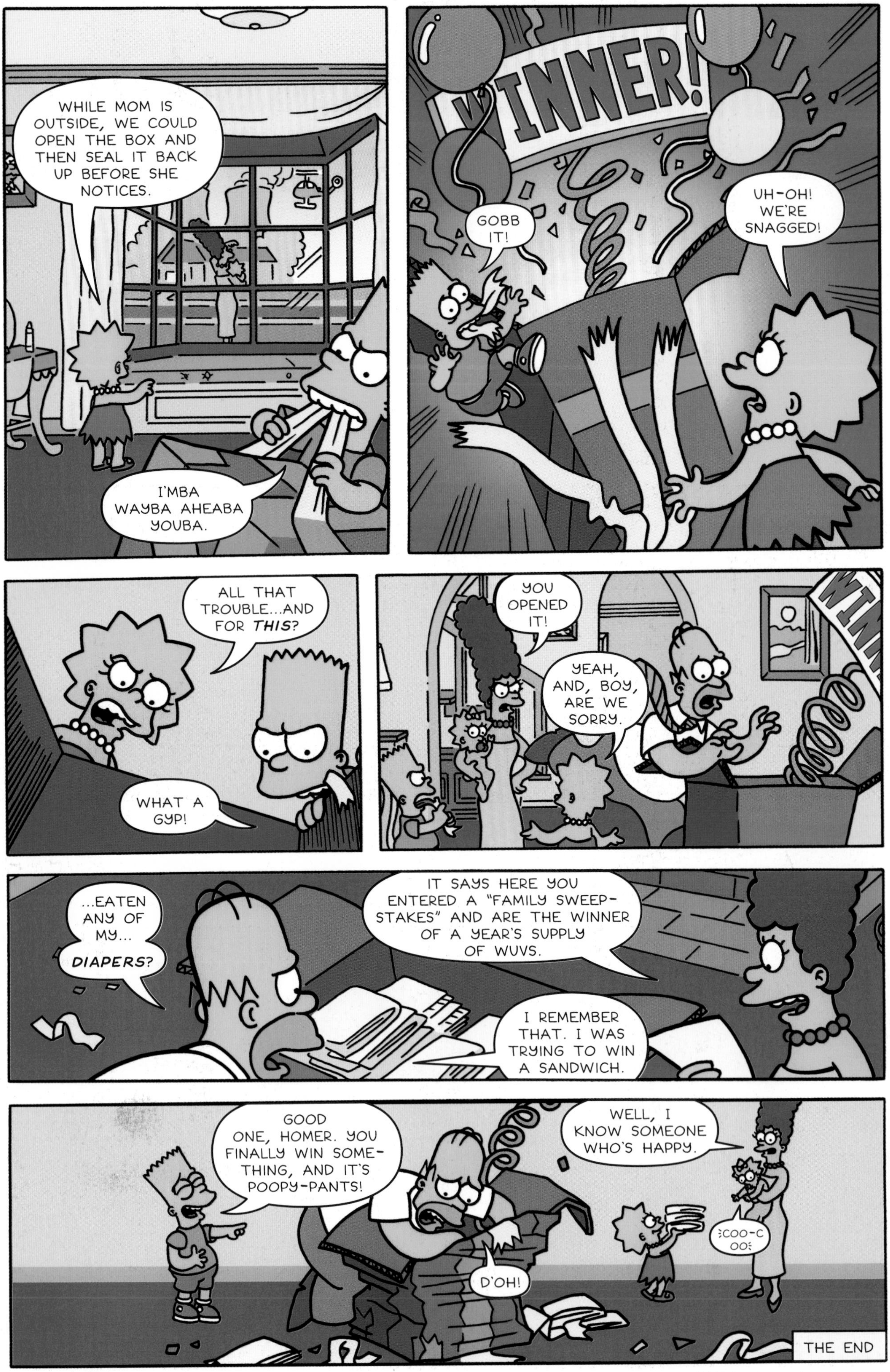
WHILE MOM IS OUTSIDE, WE COULD OPEN THE BOX AND THEN SEAL IT BACK UP BEFORE SHE NOTICES.
I'MBA WAYBA AHEABA YOUBA.
WINNER!
GOBB IT!
UH-OH! WE'RE SNAGGED!
ALL THAT TROUBLE...AND FOR *THIS?*
WHAT A GYP!
YOU OPENED IT!
YEAH, AND, BOY, ARE WE SORRY.
...EATEN ANY OF MY... *DIAPERS?*
IT SAYS HERE YOU ENTERED A "FAMILY SWEEP-STAKES" AND ARE THE WINNER OF A YEAR'S SUPPLY OF WUVS.
I REMEMBER THAT. I WAS TRYING TO WIN A SANDWICH.
GOOD ONE, HOMER. YOU FINALLY WIN SOME-THING, AND IT'S POOPY-PANTS!
WELL, I KNOW SOMEONE WHO'S HAPPY.
COO-COO
D'OH!
THE END

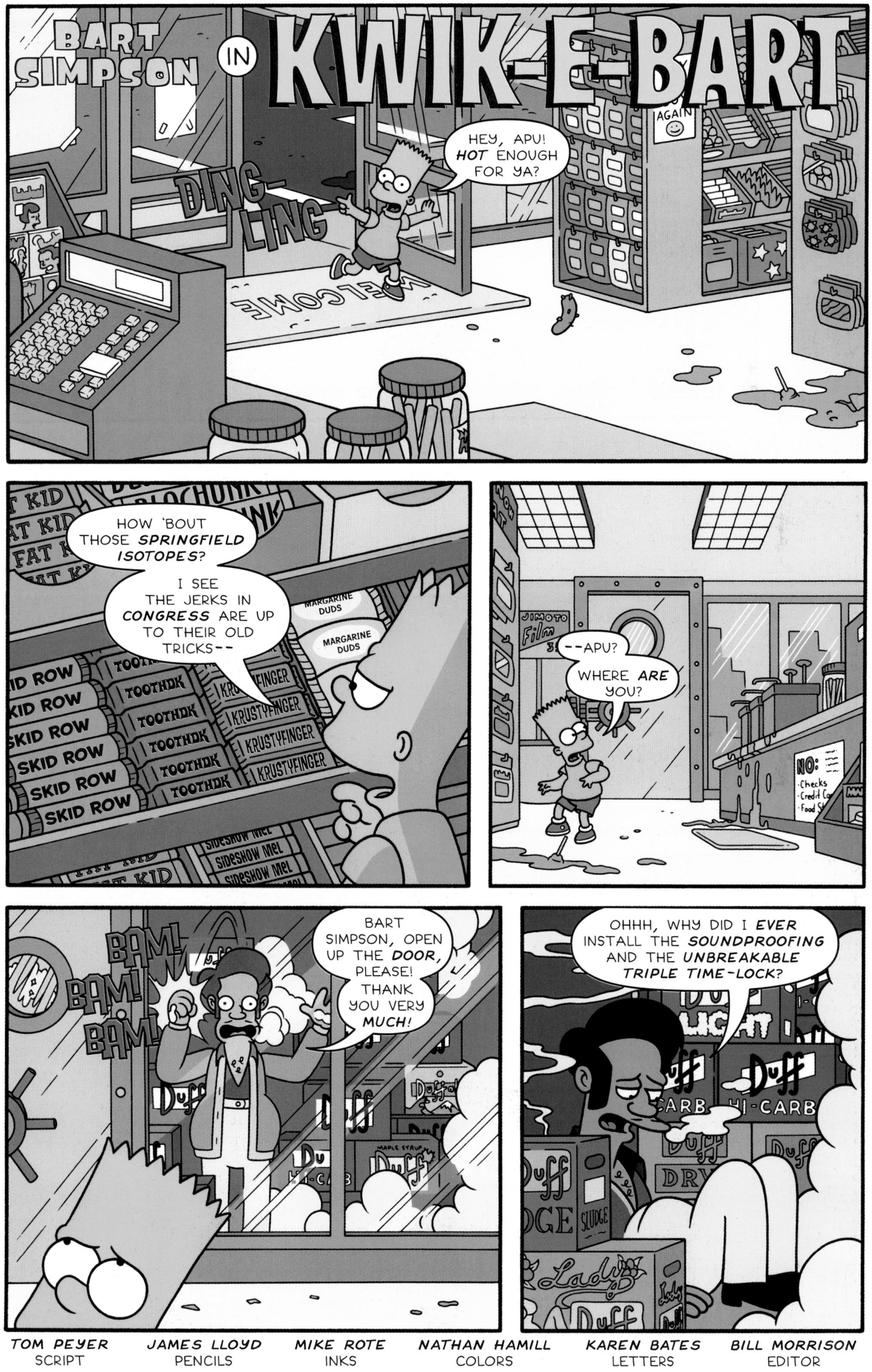
BART SIMPSON IN KWIK-E-BART
AGAIN
HEY, APU! HOT ENOUGH FOR YA?
DING-LING
WELCOME
HOW 'BOUT THOSE SPRINGFIELD ISOTOPES?
I SEE THE JERKS IN CONGRESS ARE UP TO THEIR OLD TRICKS--
MARGARINE DUDS
SKID ROW
TOOTHDK
KRUSTYFINGER
SIDESHOW MEL
FAT KID
--APU?
WHERE ARE YOU?
NO:
Checks
BAM! BAM! BAM!
BART SIMPSON, OPEN UP THE DOOR, PLEASE! THANK YOU VERY MUCH!
OHHH, WHY DID I EVER INSTALL THE SOUNDPROOFING AND THE UNBREAKABLE TRIPLE TIME-LOCK?
Duff
HI-CARB
SLUDGE
MAPLE SYRUP

TOM PEYER SCRIPT | *JAMES LLOYD* PENCILS | *MIKE ROTE* INKS | *NATHAN HAMILL* COLORS | *KAREN BATES* LETTERS | *BILL MORRISON* EDITOR

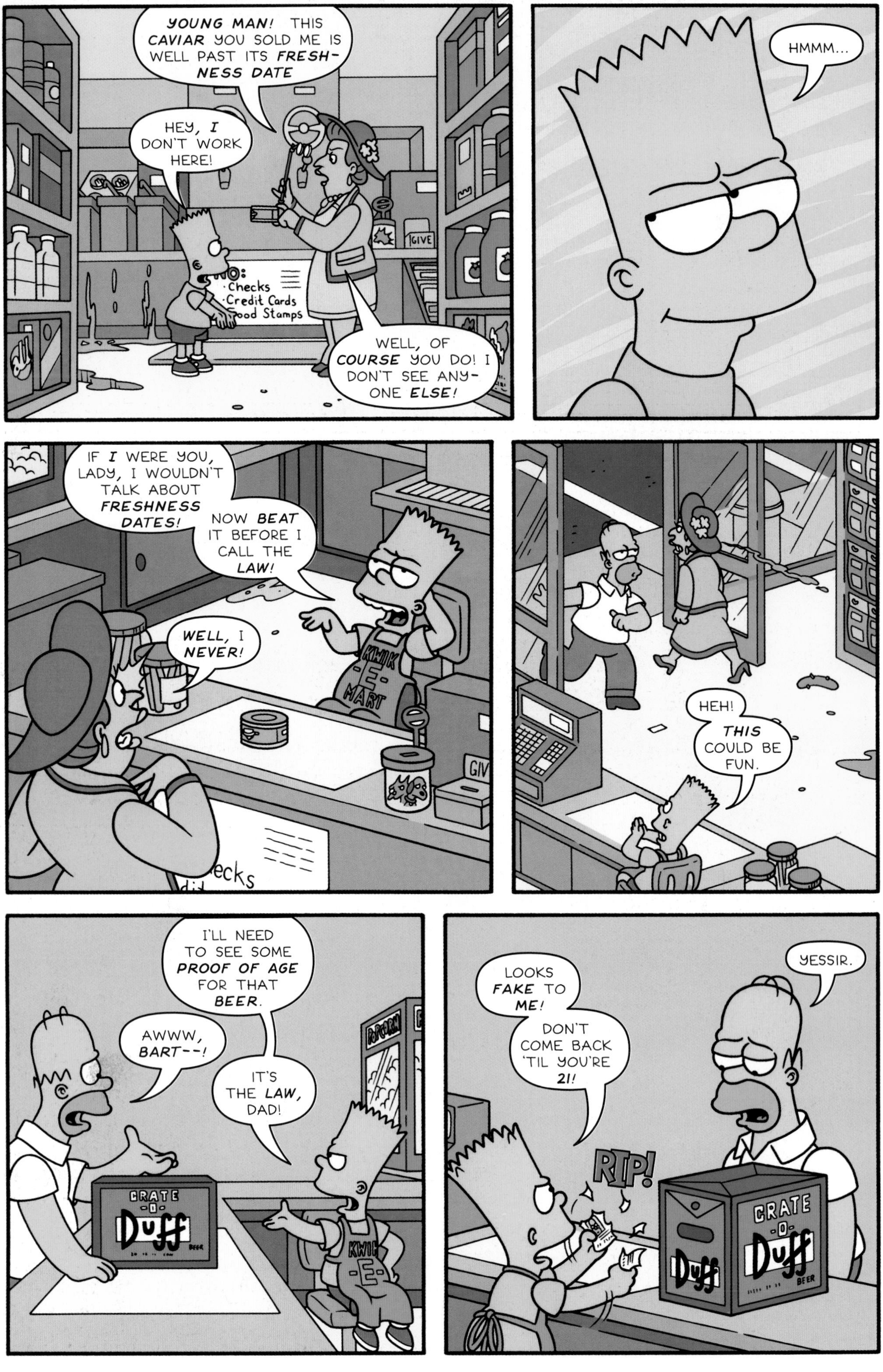
YOUNG MAN! THIS CAVIAR YOU SOLD ME IS WELL PAST ITS FRESHNESS DATE
HEY, I DON'T WORK HERE!
Checks
Credit Cards
Food Stamps
GIVE
WELL, OF COURSE YOU DO! I DON'T SEE ANYONE ELSE!
HMMM...
IF I WERE YOU, LADY, I WOULDN'T TALK ABOUT FRESHNESS DATES!
NOW BEAT IT BEFORE I CALL THE LAW!
WELL, I NEVER!
KWIK E MART
HEH! THIS COULD BE FUN.
I'LL NEED TO SEE SOME PROOF OF AGE FOR THAT BEER.
AWWW, BART--!
IT'S THE LAW, DAD!
CRATE -O- DUFF
LOOKS FAKE TO ME!
DON'T COME BACK 'TIL YOU'RE 21!
YESSIR.
RIP!
CRATE -O- DUFF BEER

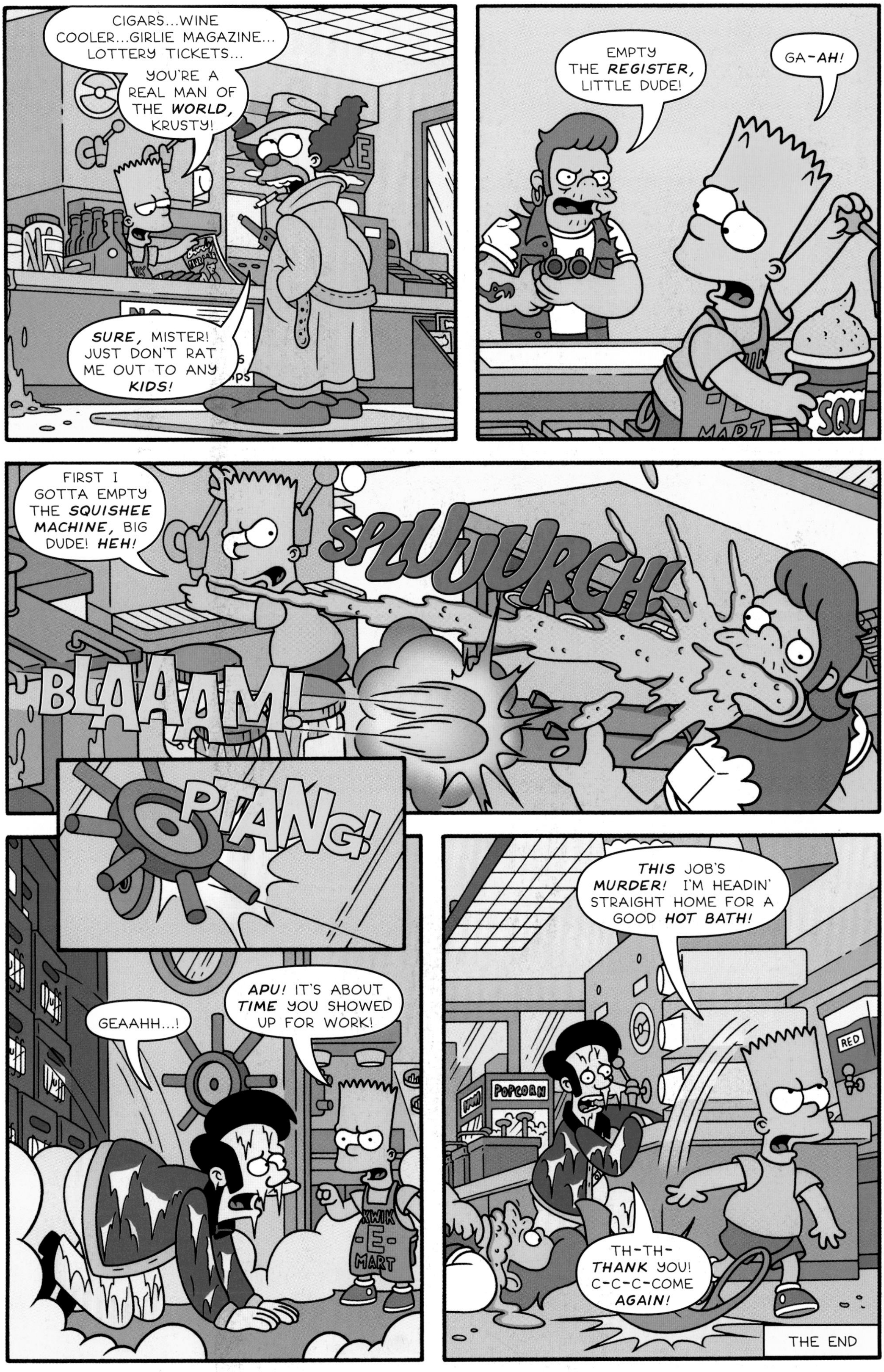
CIGARS...WINE COOLER...GIRLIE MAGAZINE... LOTTERY TICKETS...
YOU'RE A REAL MAN OF THE WORLD, KRUSTY!
SURE, MISTER! JUST DON'T RAT ME OUT TO ANY KIDS!
EMPTY THE REGISTER, LITTLE DUDE!
GA-AH!
FIRST I GOTTA EMPTY THE SQUISHEE MACHINE, BIG DUDE! HEH!
SPLUUURCH!
BLAAAM!
PTANG!
GEAAHH...!
APU! IT'S ABOUT TIME YOU SHOWED UP FOR WORK!
KWIK E MART
THIS JOB'S MURDER! I'M HEADIN' STRAIGHT HOME FOR A GOOD HOT BATH!
POPCORN
RED
TH-TH-THANK YOU! C-C-C-COME AGAIN!
THE END

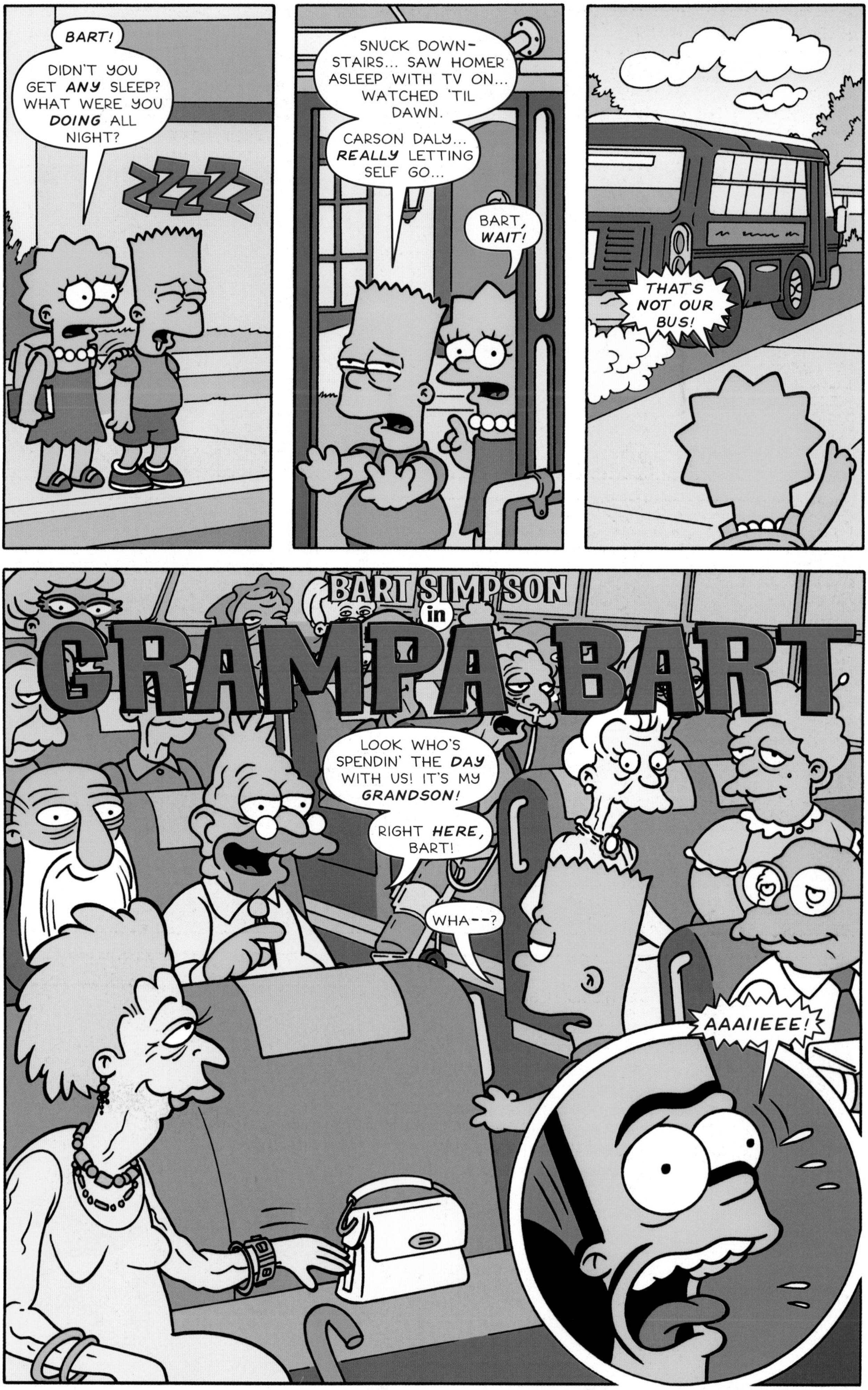
BART!
DIDN'T YOU GET ANY SLEEP? WHAT WERE YOU DOING ALL NIGHT?
ZZZZZ
SNUCK DOWN-STAIRS... SAW HOMER ASLEEP WITH TV ON... WATCHED 'TIL DAWN.
CARSON DALY... REALLY LETTING SELF GO...
BART, WAIT!
THAT'S NOT OUR BUS!
BART SIMPSON in
GRAMPA BART
LOOK WHO'S SPENDIN' THE DAY WITH US! IT'S MY GRANDSON!
RIGHT HERE, BART!
WHA--?
AAAIIEEE!

TOM PEYER SCRIPT · JOHN COSTANZA PENCILS · HOWARD SHUM INKS · ART VILLANUEVA COLORS · KAREN BATES LETTERS · BILL MORRISON EDITOR

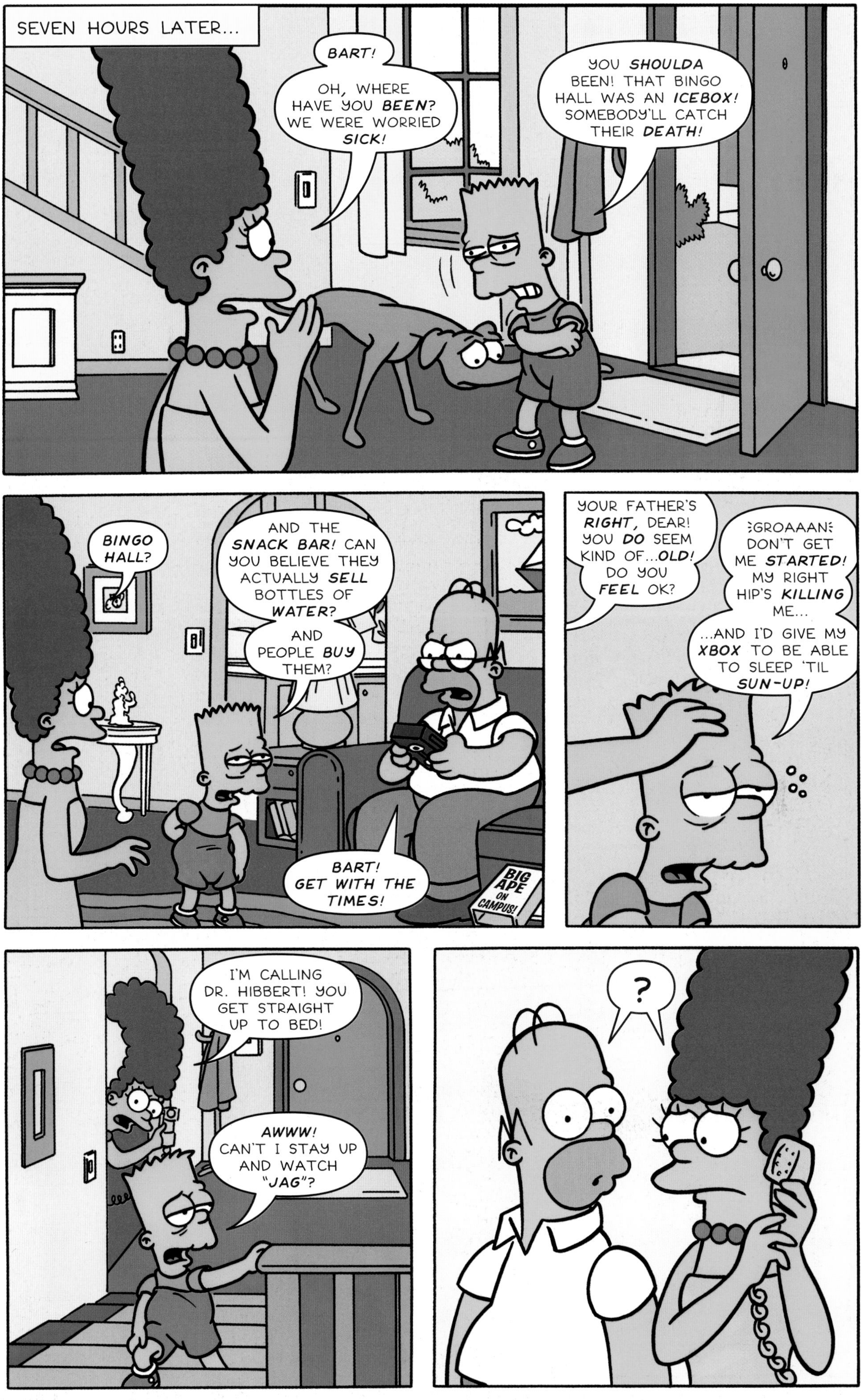
SEVEN HOURS LATER...
BART!
OH, WHERE HAVE YOU BEEN? WE WERE WORRIED SICK!
YOU SHOULDA BEEN! THAT BINGO HALL WAS AN ICEBOX! SOMEBODY'LL CATCH THEIR DEATH!
BINGO HALL?
AND THE SNACK BAR! CAN YOU BELIEVE THEY ACTUALLY SELL BOTTLES OF WATER?
AND PEOPLE BUY THEM?
BART! GET WITH THE TIMES!
BIG APE ON CAMPUS!
YOUR FATHER'S RIGHT, DEAR! YOU DO SEEM KIND OF...OLD! DO YOU FEEL OK?
GROAAAN DON'T GET ME STARTED! MY RIGHT HIP'S KILLING ME...
...AND I'D GIVE MY XBOX TO BE ABLE TO SLEEP 'TIL SUN-UP!
I'M CALLING DR. HIBBERT! YOU GET STRAIGHT UP TO BED!
AWWW! CAN'T I STAY UP AND WATCH "JAG"?
?

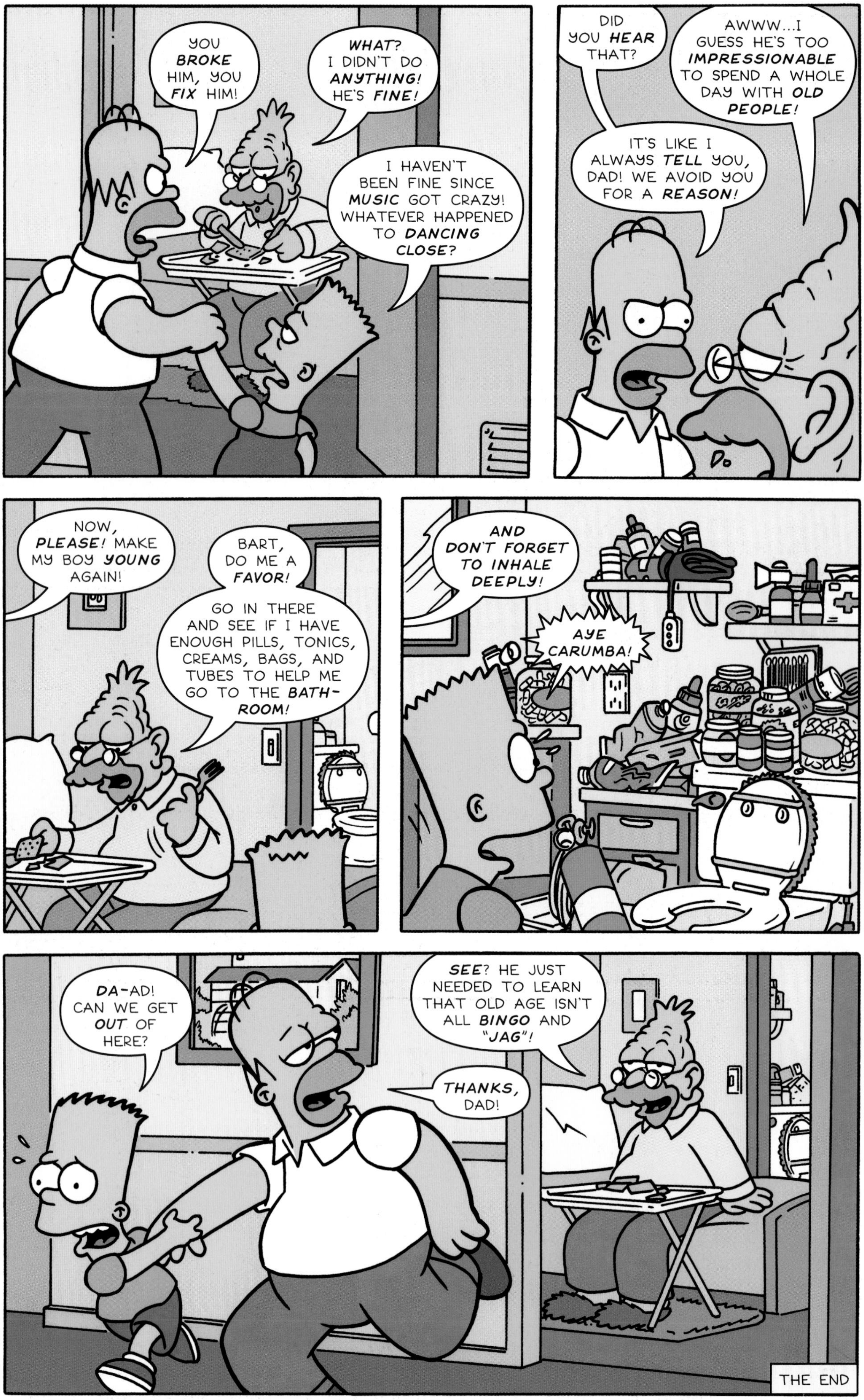
YOU BROKE HIM, YOU FIX HIM!
WHAT? I DIDN'T DO ANYTHING! HE'S FINE!
I HAVEN'T BEEN FINE SINCE MUSIC GOT CRAZY! WHATEVER HAPPENED TO DANCING CLOSE?
DID YOU HEAR THAT?
AWWW...I GUESS HE'S TOO IMPRESSIONABLE TO SPEND A WHOLE DAY WITH OLD PEOPLE!
IT'S LIKE I ALWAYS TELL YOU, DAD! WE AVOID YOU FOR A REASON!
NOW, PLEASE! MAKE MY BOY YOUNG AGAIN!
BART, DO ME A FAVOR!
GO IN THERE AND SEE IF I HAVE ENOUGH PILLS, TONICS, CREAMS, BAGS, AND TUBES TO HELP ME GO TO THE BATH-ROOM!
AND DON'T FORGET TO INHALE DEEPLY!
AYE CARUMBA!
DA-AD! CAN WE GET OUT OF HERE?
SEE? HE JUST NEEDED TO LEARN THAT OLD AGE ISN'T ALL BINGO AND "JAG"!
THANKS, DAD!
THE END

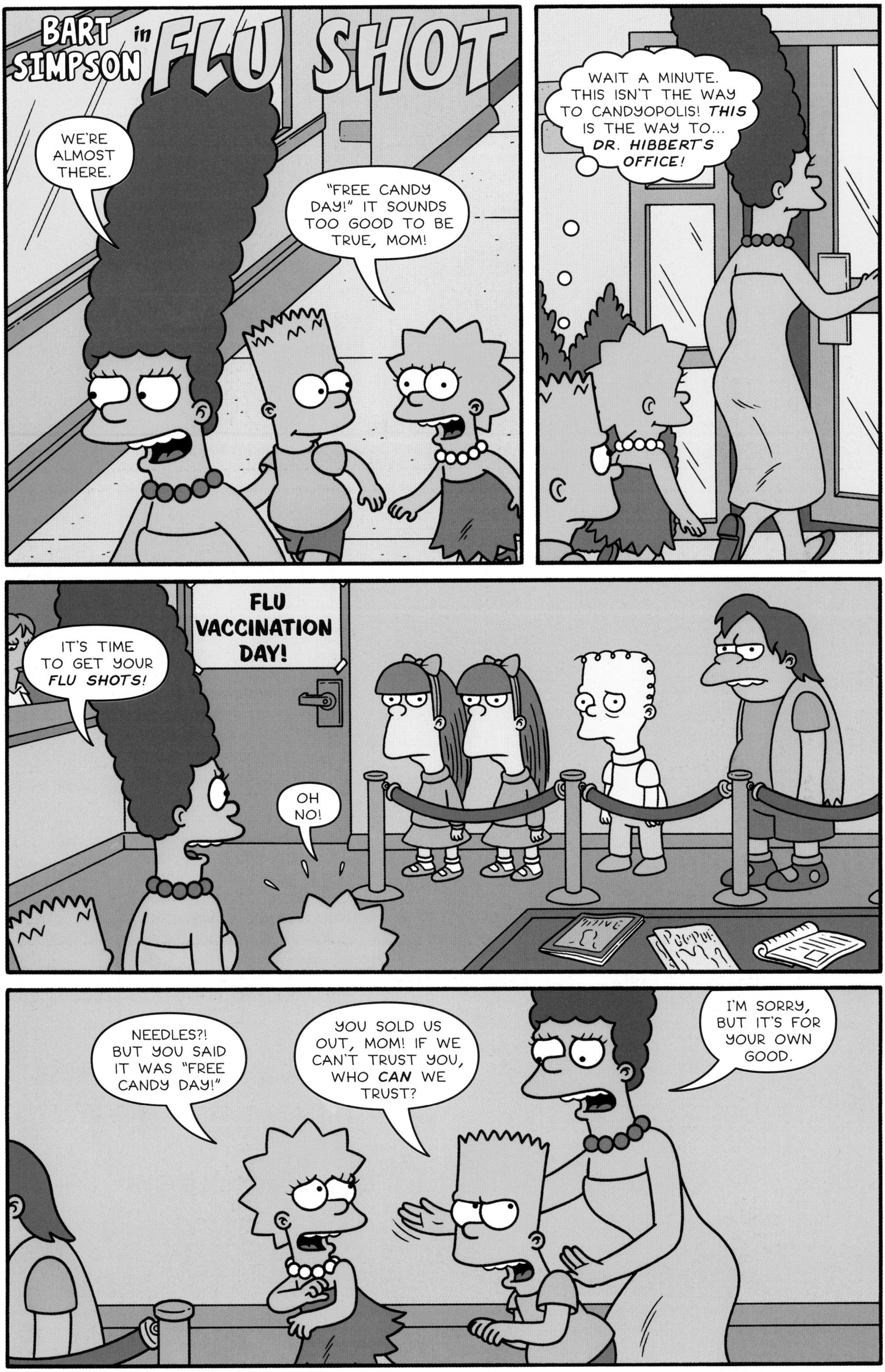
BART SIMPSON in FLU SHOT
WE'RE ALMOST THERE.
"FREE CANDY DAY!" IT SOUNDS TOO GOOD TO BE TRUE, MOM!
WAIT A MINUTE. THIS ISN'T THE WAY TO CANDYOPOLIS! THIS IS THE WAY TO... DR. HIBBERT'S OFFICE!
FLU VACCINATION DAY!
IT'S TIME TO GET YOUR FLU SHOTS!
OH NO!
NEEDLES?! BUT YOU SAID IT WAS "FREE CANDY DAY!"
YOU SOLD US OUT, MOM! IF WE CAN'T TRUST YOU, WHO CAN WE TRUST?
I'M SORRY, BUT IT'S FOR YOUR OWN GOOD.

JAMES BATES SCRIPT — *JASON HO* PENCILS — *MIKE ROTE* INKS — *NATHAN HAMILL* COLORS — *KAREN BATES* LETTERS — *BILL MORRISON* EDITOR

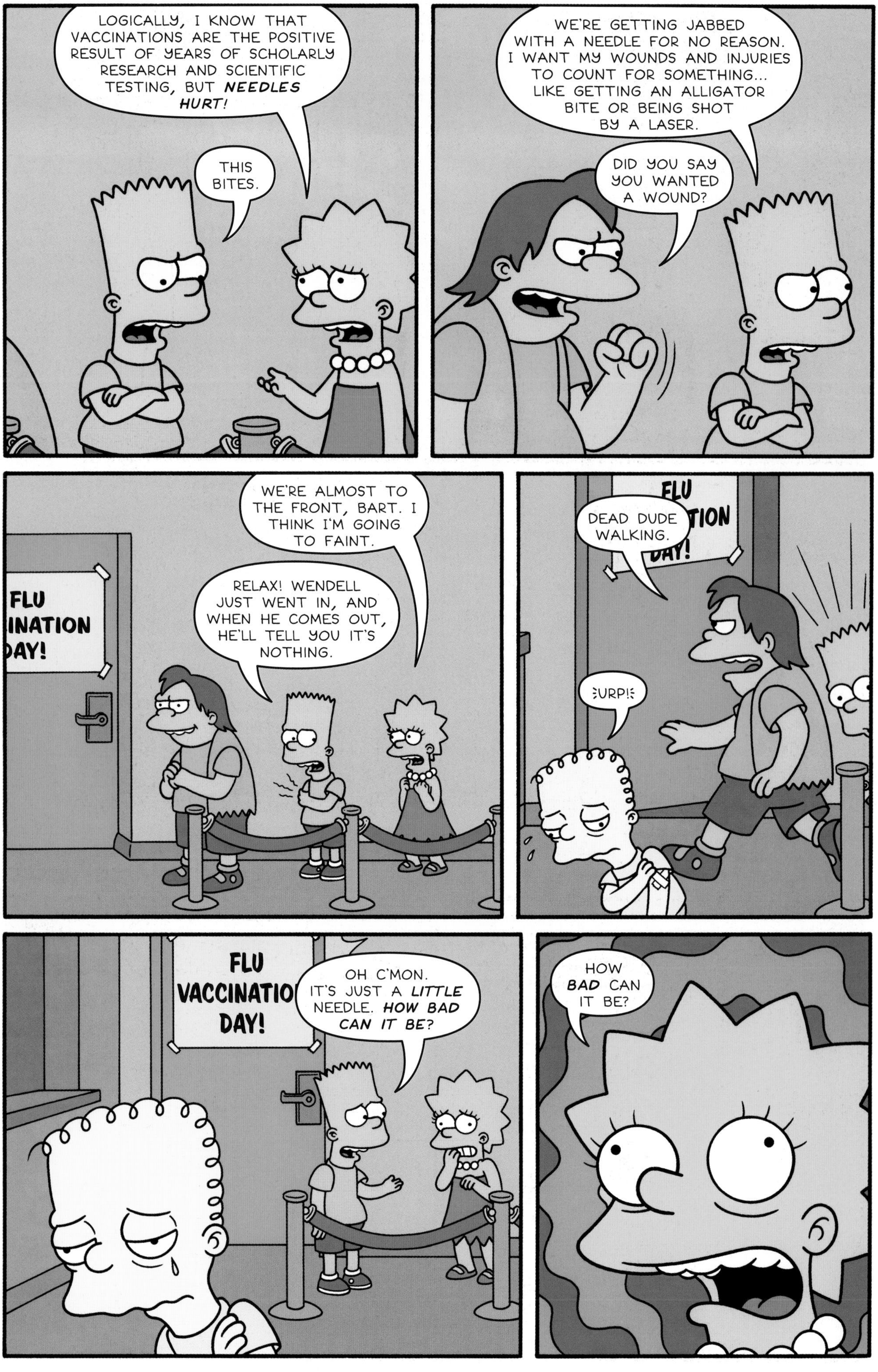
LOGICALLY, I KNOW THAT VACCINATIONS ARE THE POSITIVE RESULT OF YEARS OF SCHOLARLY RESEARCH AND SCIENTIFIC TESTING, BUT NEEDLES HURT!
THIS BITES.
WE'RE GETTING JABBED WITH A NEEDLE FOR NO REASON. I WANT MY WOUNDS AND INJURIES TO COUNT FOR SOMETHING... LIKE GETTING AN ALLIGATOR BITE OR BEING SHOT BY A LASER.
DID YOU SAY YOU WANTED A WOUND?
WE'RE ALMOST TO THE FRONT, BART. I THINK I'M GOING TO FAINT.
RELAX! WENDELL JUST WENT IN, AND WHEN HE COMES OUT, HE'LL TELL YOU IT'S NOTHING.
DEAD DUDE WALKING.
URP!
FLU VACCINATIO DAY!
OH C'MON. IT'S JUST A LITTLE NEEDLE. HOW BAD CAN IT BE?
HOW BAD CAN IT BE?

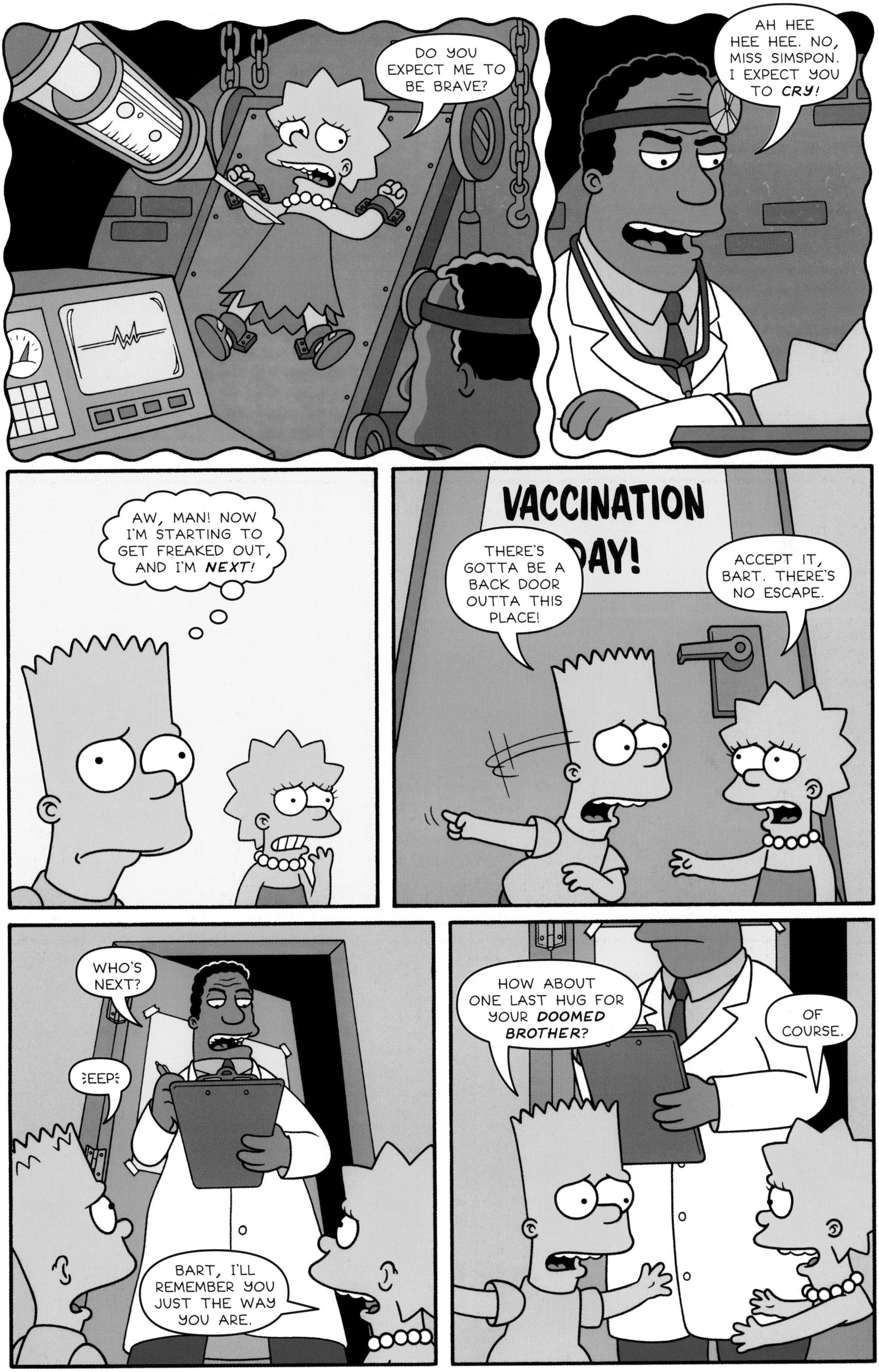
DO YOU EXPECT ME TO BE BRAVE?
AH HEE HEE HEE. NO, MISS SIMSPON. I EXPECT YOU TO *CRY*!
AW, MAN! NOW I'M STARTING TO GET FREAKED OUT, AND I'M *NEXT*!
VACCINATION DAY!
THERE'S GOTTA BE A BACK DOOR OUTTA THIS PLACE!
ACCEPT IT, BART. THERE'S NO ESCAPE.
WHO'S NEXT?
EEP
BART, I'LL REMEMBER YOU JUST THE WAY YOU ARE.
HOW ABOUT ONE LAST HUG FOR YOUR *DOOMED BROTHER*?
OF COURSE.

SUCKER! THE PATENTED *SPIN-O-RAMA!*

HUH? WHAT ARE YOU--?!

AH, IT LOOKS LIKE YOU'RE NEXT IN LINE, LISA.

I FEEL BAD FOR YOU. *I REALLY, REALLY DO.*

YOU TRICKED ME!

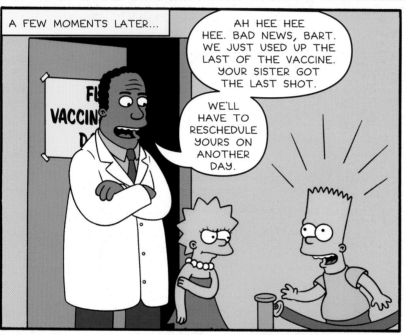

A FEW MOMENTS LATER...

AH HEE HEE HEE. BAD NEWS, BART. WE JUST USED UP THE LAST OF THE VACCINE. YOUR SISTER GOT THE LAST SHOT.

WE'LL HAVE TO RESCHEDULE YOURS ON ANOTHER DAY.

FLU VACCIN...D...

WOO-HOO!

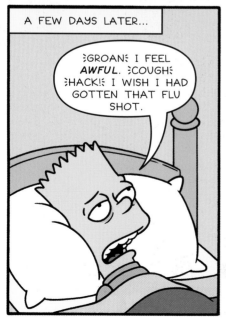

A FEW DAYS LATER...

:GROAN: I FEEL *AWFUL.* :COUGH: :HACK!: I WISH I HAD GOTTEN THAT FLU SHOT.

WHERE IS EVERYONE GOING?

TODAY REALLY *IS* "FREE CANDY DAY" AT CANDYOPOLIS, BUT NOW THAT YOU HAVE THE FLU, YOU HAVE TO STAY HOME IN BED. SORRY.

I FEEL BAD FOR YOU, BART. *I REALLY, REALLY DO!*

THE END

32

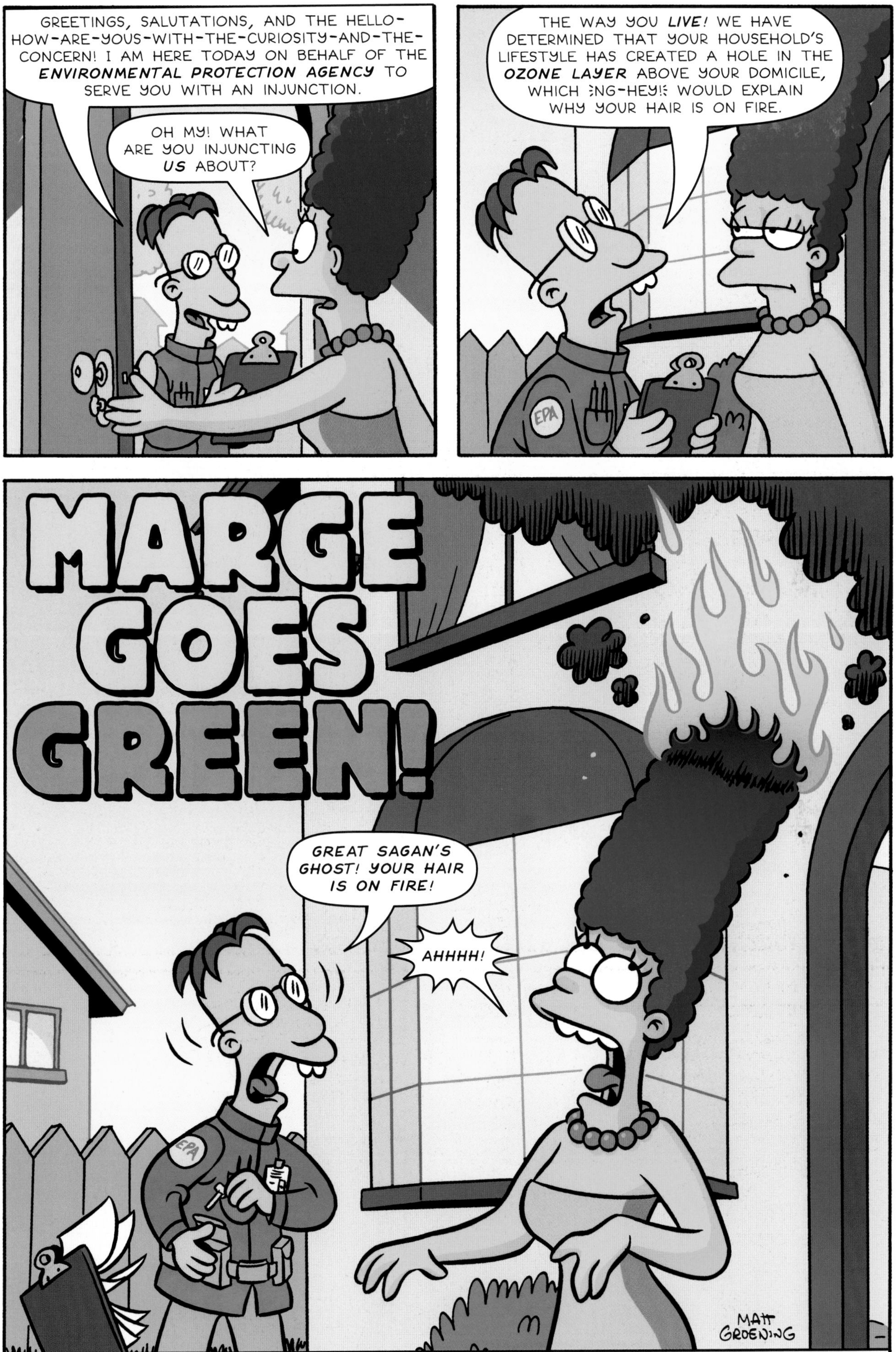
GREETINGS, SALUTATIONS, AND THE HELLO-HOW-ARE-YOUS-WITH-THE-CURIOSITY-AND-THE-CONCERN! I AM HERE TODAY ON BEHALF OF THE ENVIRONMENTAL PROTECTION AGENCY TO SERVE YOU WITH AN INJUNCTION.
OH MY! WHAT ARE YOU INJUNCTING US ABOUT?
THE WAY YOU LIVE! WE HAVE DETERMINED THAT YOUR HOUSEHOLD'S LIFESTYLE HAS CREATED A HOLE IN THE OZONE LAYER ABOVE YOUR DOMICILE, WHICH NG-HEY! WOULD EXPLAIN WHY YOUR HAIR IS ON FIRE.
EPA
MARGE GOES GREEN!
GREAT SAGAN'S GHOST! YOUR HAIR IS ON FIRE!
AHHHH!
EPA
MATT GROENING

SCOTT M. GIMPLE
SCRIPT

MIKE KAZALEH
PENCILS & INKS

ART VILLANUEVA
COLORS

KAREN BATES
LETTERS

BILL MORRISON
EDITOR

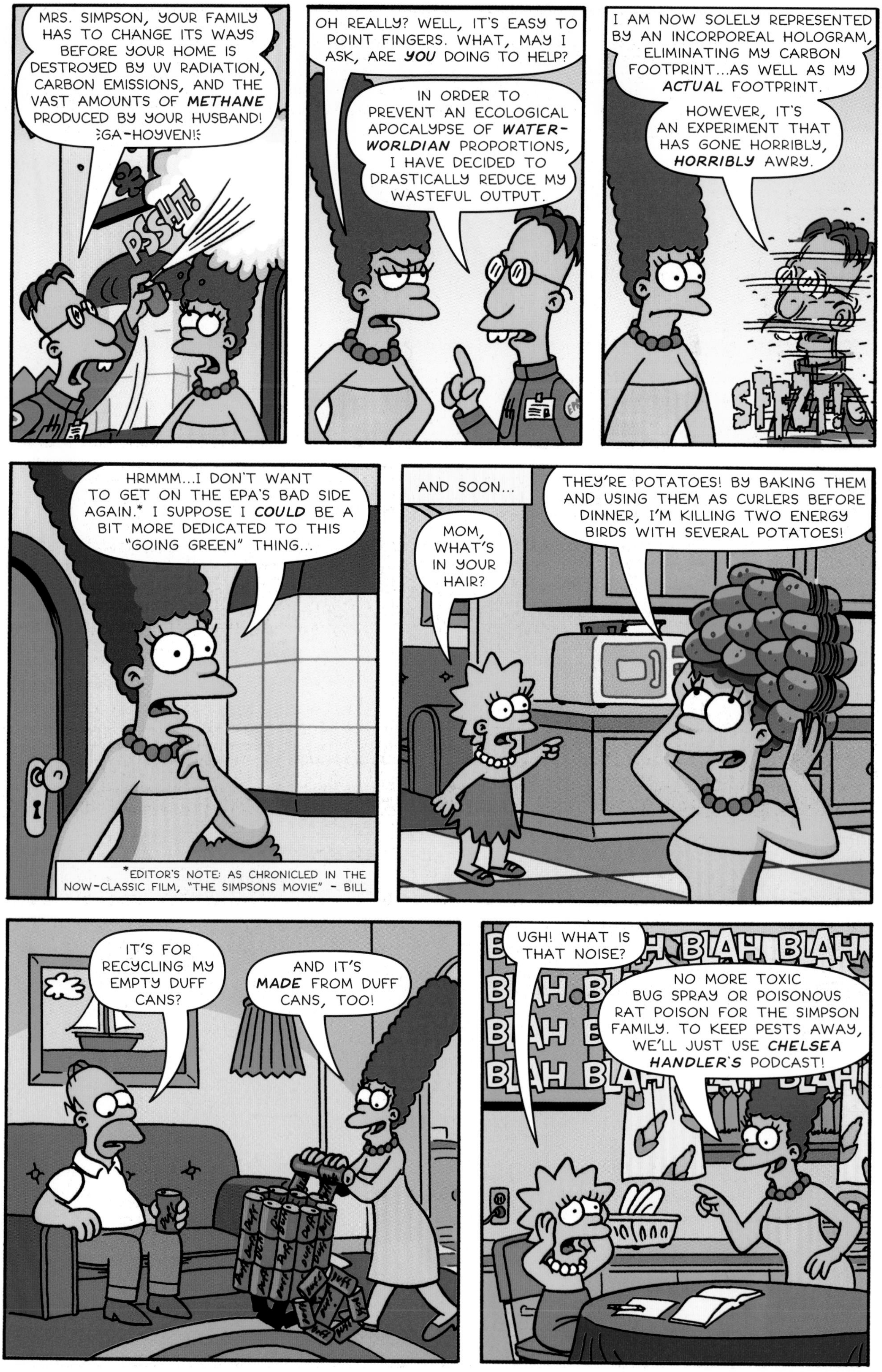
MRS. SIMPSON, YOUR FAMILY HAS TO CHANGE ITS WAYS BEFORE YOUR HOME IS DESTROYED BY UV RADIATION, CARBON EMISSIONS, AND THE VAST AMOUNTS OF **METHANE** PRODUCED BY YOUR HUSBAND! GA-HOYVEN!
PSSHT!
OH REALLY? WELL, IT'S EASY TO POINT FINGERS. WHAT, MAY I ASK, ARE **YOU** DOING TO HELP?
IN ORDER TO PREVENT AN ECOLOGICAL APOCALYPSE OF **WATER-WORLDIAN** PROPORTIONS, I HAVE DECIDED TO DRASTICALLY REDUCE MY WASTEFUL OUTPUT.
EPA
I AM NOW SOLELY REPRESENTED BY AN INCORPOREAL HOLOGRAM, ELIMINATING MY CARBON FOOTPRINT...AS WELL AS MY **ACTUAL** FOOTPRINT.
HOWEVER, IT'S AN EXPERIMENT THAT HAS GONE HORRIBLY, **HORRIBLY** AWRY.
SFFZT!
HRMMM...I DON'T WANT TO GET ON THE EPA'S BAD SIDE AGAIN.* I SUPPOSE I **COULD** BE A BIT MORE DEDICATED TO THIS "GOING GREEN" THING...
*EDITOR'S NOTE: AS CHRONICLED IN THE NOW-CLASSIC FILM, "THE SIMPSONS MOVIE" - BILL
AND SOON...
MOM, WHAT'S IN YOUR HAIR?
THEY'RE POTATOES! BY BAKING THEM AND USING THEM AS CURLERS BEFORE DINNER, I'M KILLING TWO ENERGY BIRDS WITH SEVERAL POTATOES!
IT'S FOR RECYCLING MY EMPTY DUFF CANS?
AND IT'S **MADE** FROM DUFF CANS, TOO!
DUFF
UGH! WHAT IS THAT NOISE?
BLAH BLAH BLAH
NO MORE TOXIC BUG SPRAY OR POISONOUS RAT POISON FOR THE SIMPSON FAMILY. TO KEEP PESTS AWAY, WE'LL JUST USE **CHELSEA HANDLER'S** PODCAST!

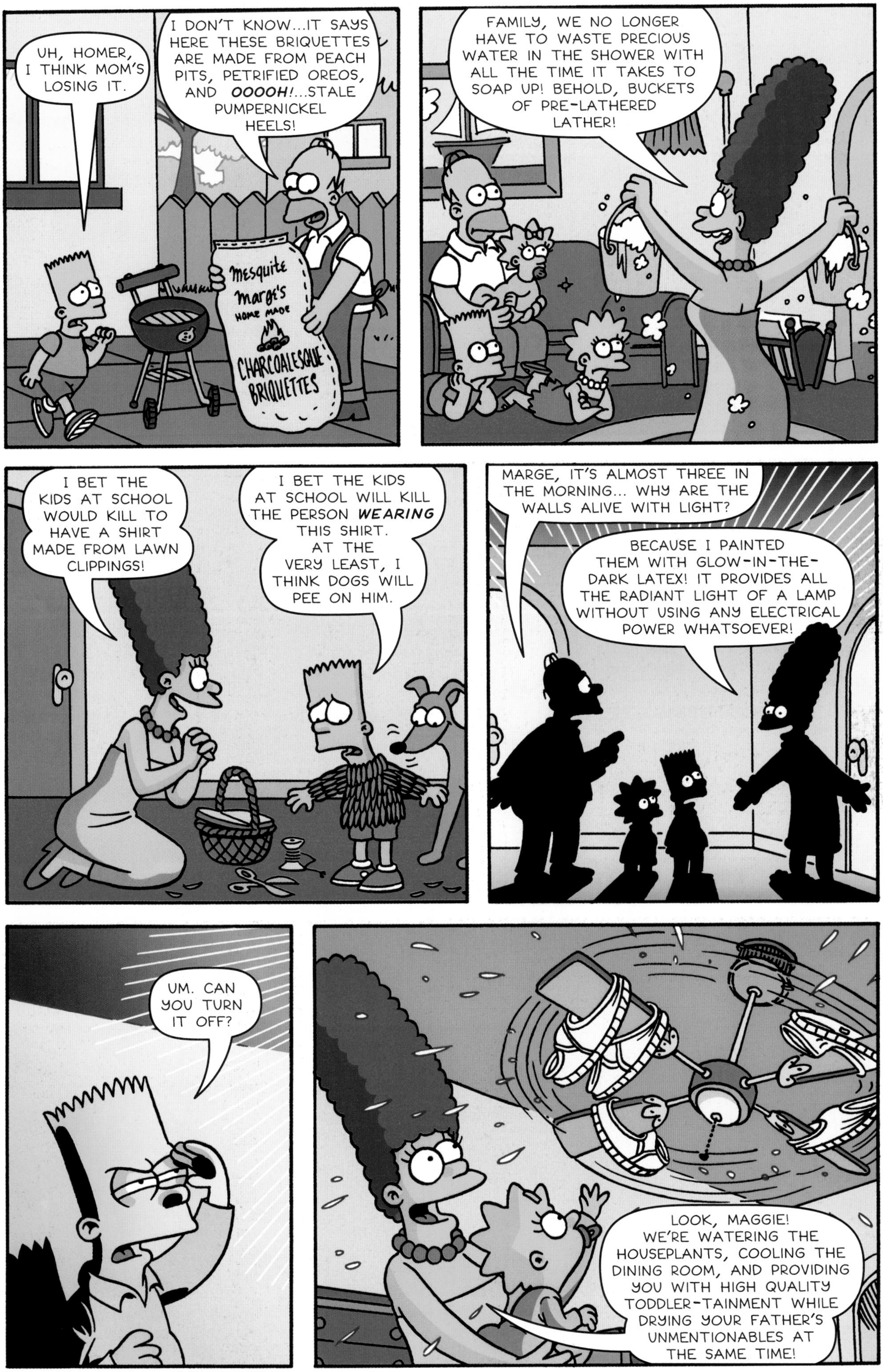
UH, HOMER, I THINK MOM'S LOSING IT.
I DON'T KNOW...IT SAYS HERE THESE BRIQUETTES ARE MADE FROM PEACH PITS, PETRIFIED OREOS, AND *OOOOH!*...STALE PUMPERNICKEL HEELS!
Mesquite Marge's Home Made CHARCOALESQUE BRIQUETTES
FAMILY, WE NO LONGER HAVE TO WASTE PRECIOUS WATER IN THE SHOWER WITH ALL THE TIME IT TAKES TO SOAP UP! BEHOLD, BUCKETS OF PRE-LATHERED LATHER!
I BET THE KIDS AT SCHOOL WOULD KILL TO HAVE A SHIRT MADE FROM LAWN CLIPPINGS!
I BET THE KIDS AT SCHOOL WILL KILL THE PERSON *WEARING* THIS SHIRT. AT THE VERY LEAST, I THINK DOGS WILL PEE ON HIM.
MARGE, IT'S ALMOST THREE IN THE MORNING... WHY ARE THE WALLS ALIVE WITH LIGHT?
BECAUSE I PAINTED THEM WITH GLOW-IN-THE-DARK LATEX! IT PROVIDES ALL THE RADIANT LIGHT OF A LAMP WITHOUT USING ANY ELECTRICAL POWER WHATSOEVER!
UM. CAN YOU TURN IT OFF?
LOOK, MAGGIE! WE'RE WATERING THE HOUSEPLANTS, COOLING THE DINING ROOM, AND PROVIDING YOU WITH HIGH QUALITY TODDLER-TAINMENT WHILE DRYING YOUR FATHER'S UNMENTIONABLES AT THE SAME TIME!

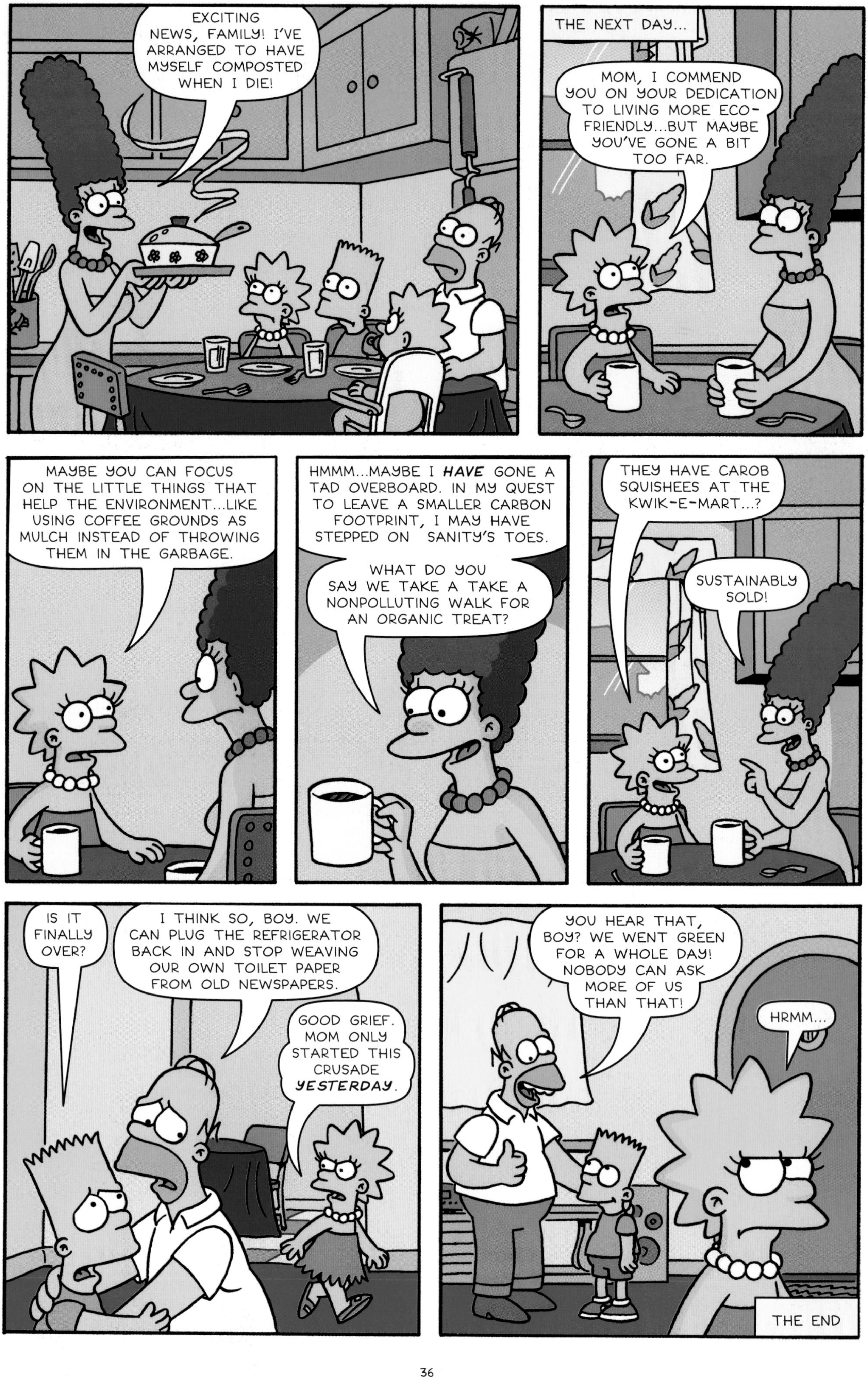
EXCITING NEWS, FAMILY! I'VE ARRANGED TO HAVE MYSELF COMPOSTED WHEN I DIE!
THE NEXT DAY...
MOM, I COMMEND YOU ON YOUR DEDICATION TO LIVING MORE ECO-FRIENDLY...BUT MAYBE YOU'VE GONE A BIT TOO FAR.
MAYBE YOU CAN FOCUS ON THE LITTLE THINGS THAT HELP THE ENVIRONMENT...LIKE USING COFFEE GROUNDS AS MULCH INSTEAD OF THROWING THEM IN THE GARBAGE.
HMMM...MAYBE I ***HAVE*** GONE A TAD OVERBOARD. IN MY QUEST TO LEAVE A SMALLER CARBON FOOTPRINT, I MAY HAVE STEPPED ON SANITY'S TOES.
WHAT DO YOU SAY WE TAKE A TAKE A NONPOLLUTING WALK FOR AN ORGANIC TREAT?
THEY HAVE CAROB SQUISHEES AT THE KWIK-E-MART...?
SUSTAINABLY SOLD!
IS IT FINALLY OVER?
I THINK SO, BOY. WE CAN PLUG THE REFRIGERATOR BACK IN AND STOP WEAVING OUR OWN TOILET PAPER FROM OLD NEWSPAPERS.
GOOD GRIEF. MOM ONLY STARTED THIS CRUSADE ***YESTERDAY***.
YOU HEAR THAT, BOY? WE WENT GREEN FOR A WHOLE DAY! NOBODY CAN ASK MORE OF US THAN THAT!
HRMM...
THE END

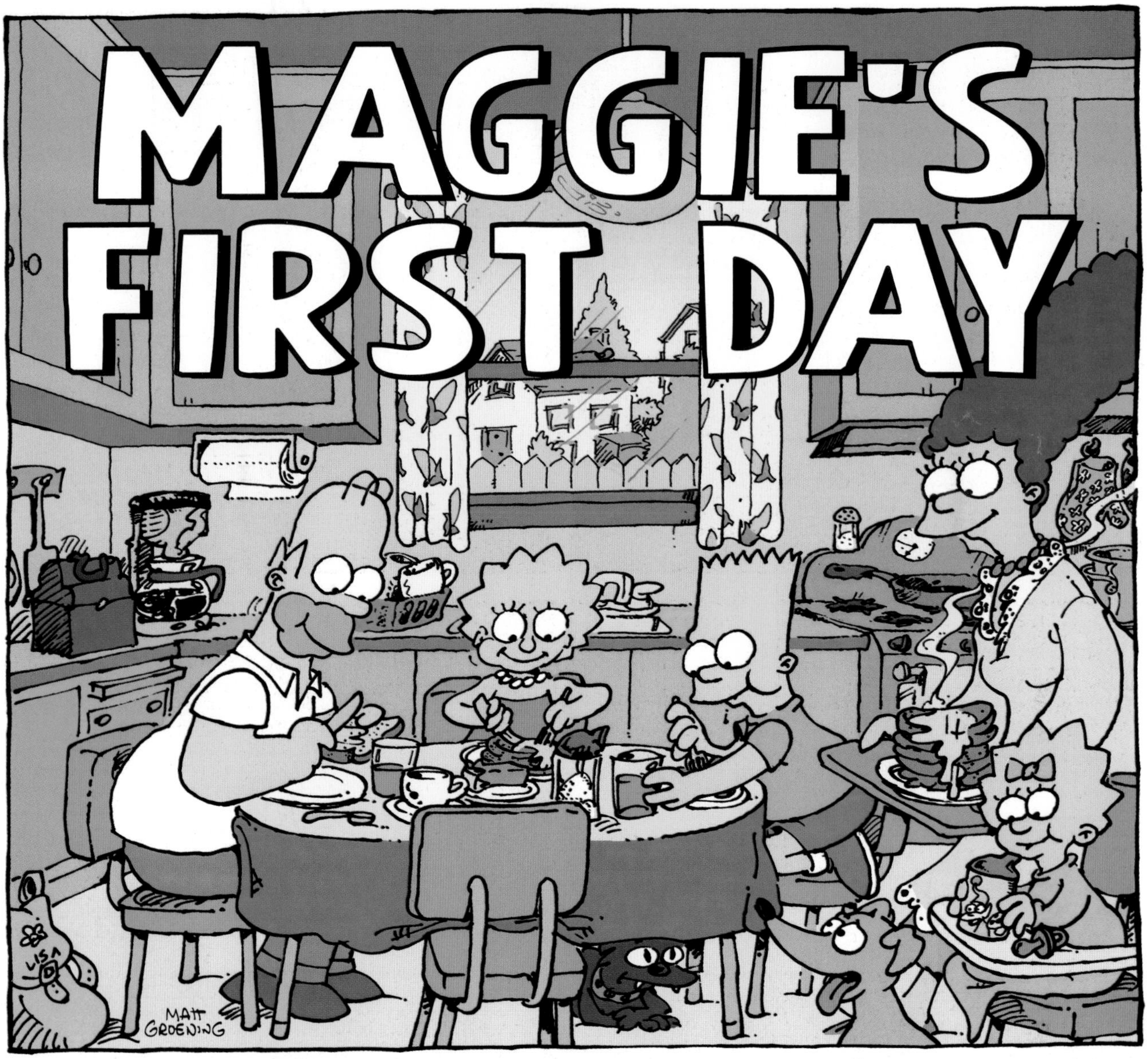
MAGGIE'S FIRST DAY
LISA
MATT GROENING

SERGIO ARAGONÉS STORY & ART
ART VILLANUEVA COLORS
BILL MORRISON EDITOR

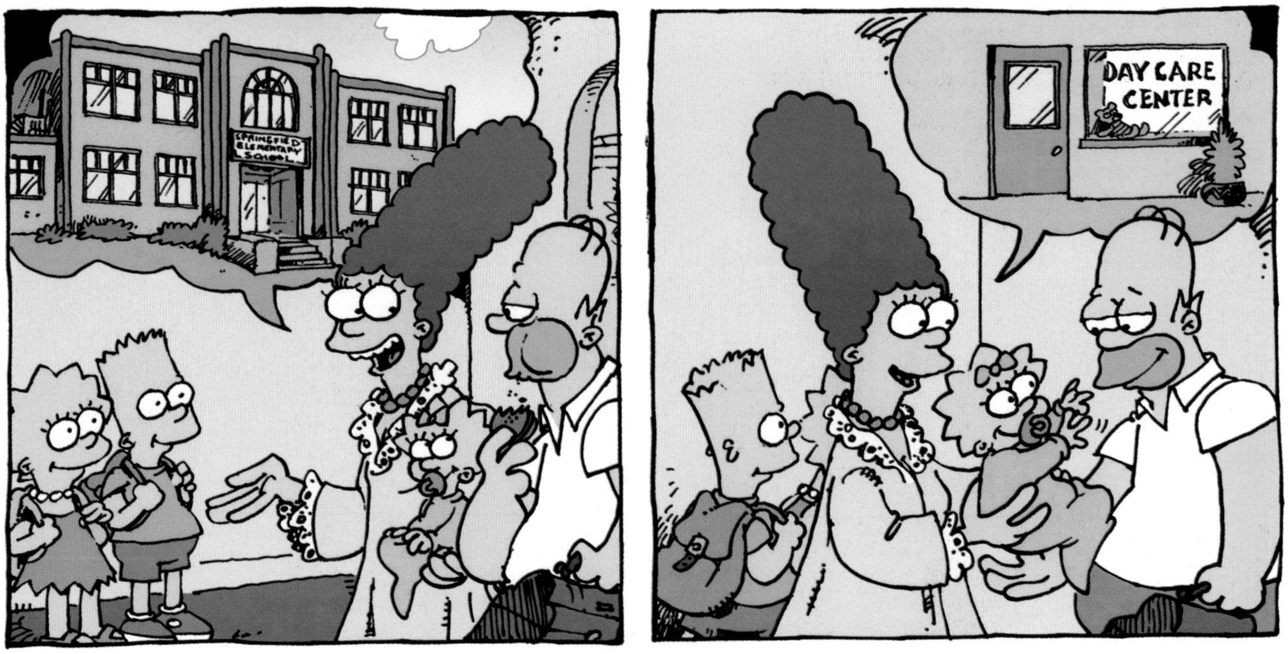
SPRINGFIELD ELEMENTARY SCHOOL
DAY CARE CENTER

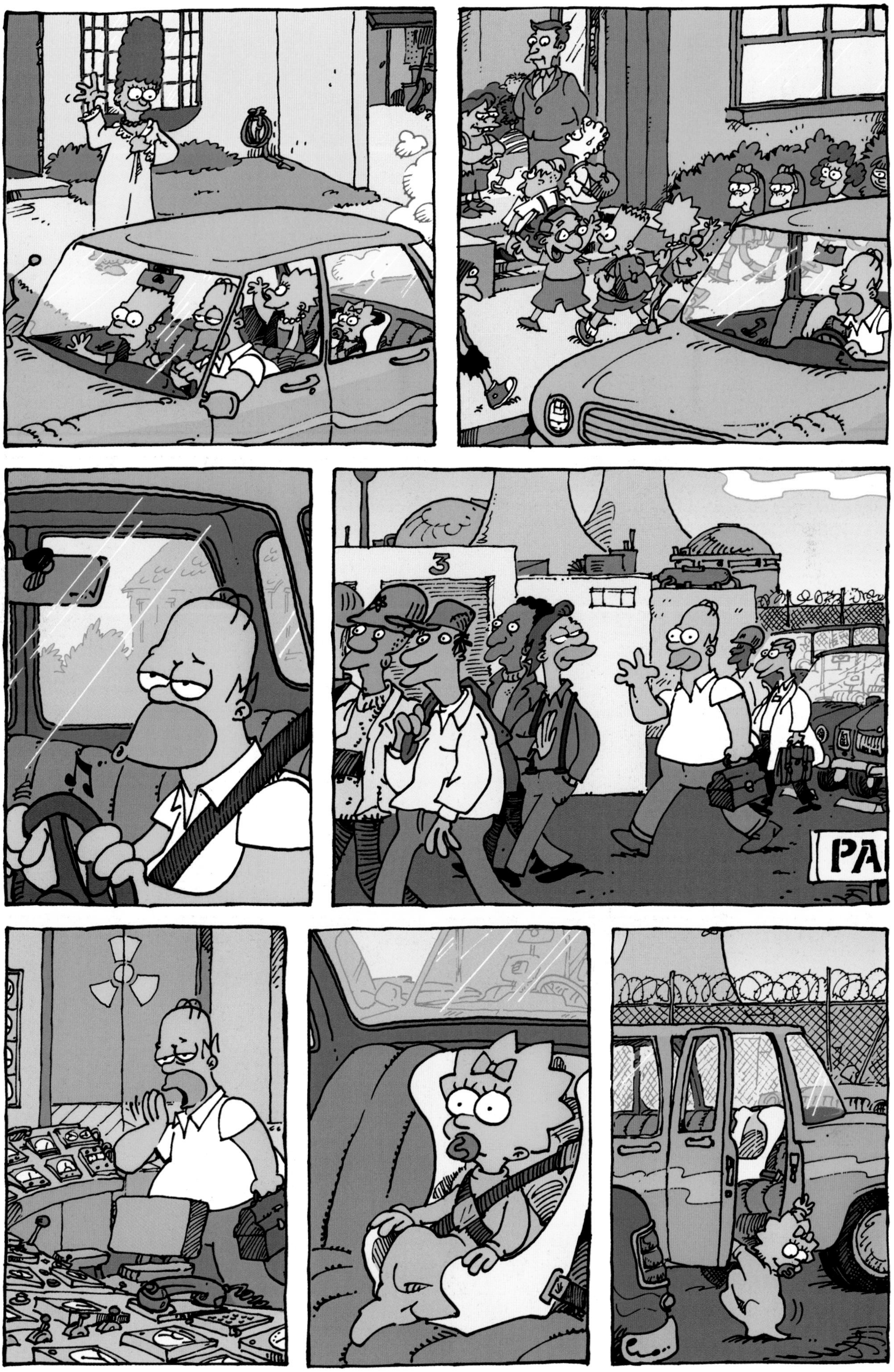
3
PA

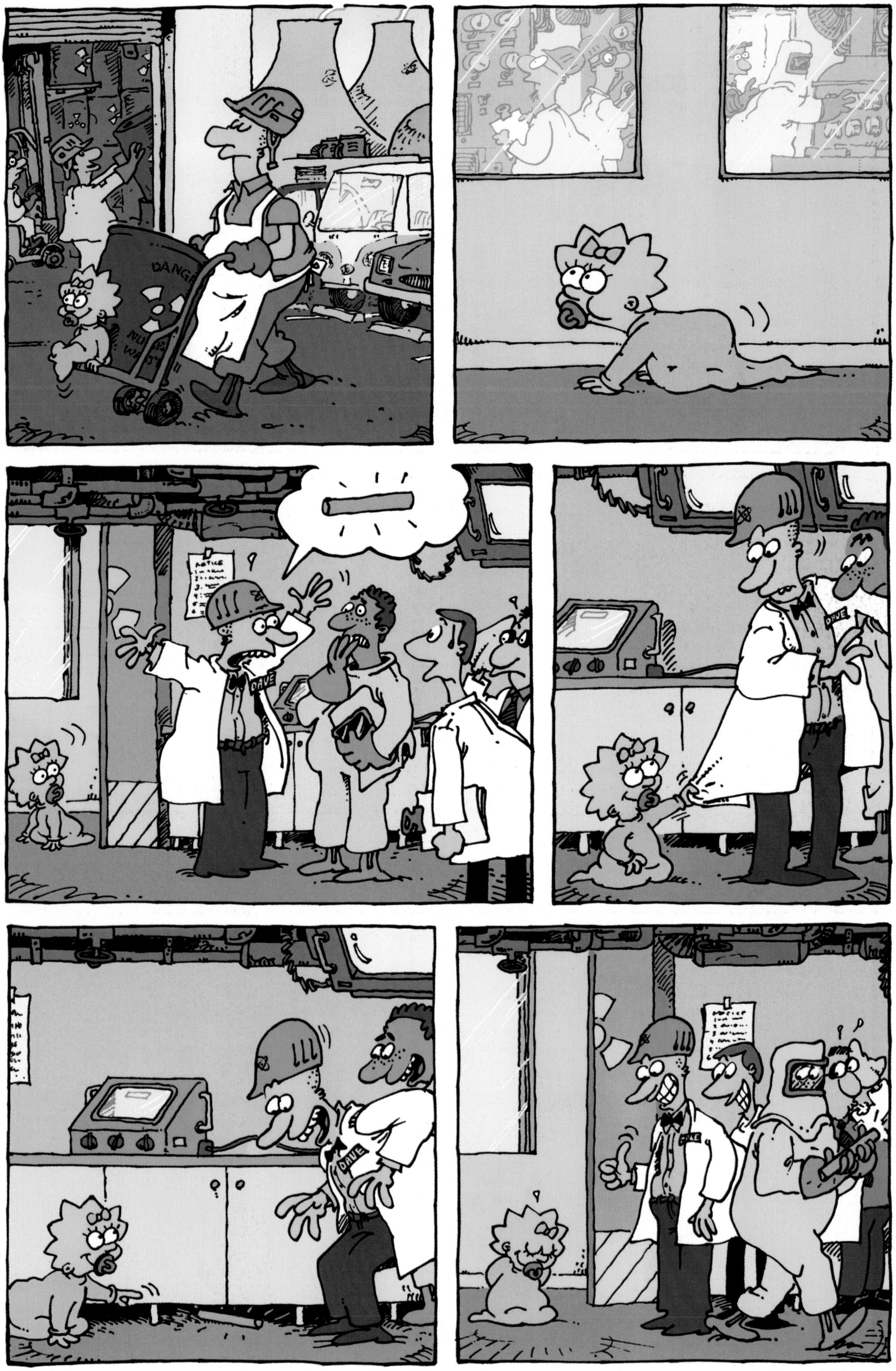
DAVE

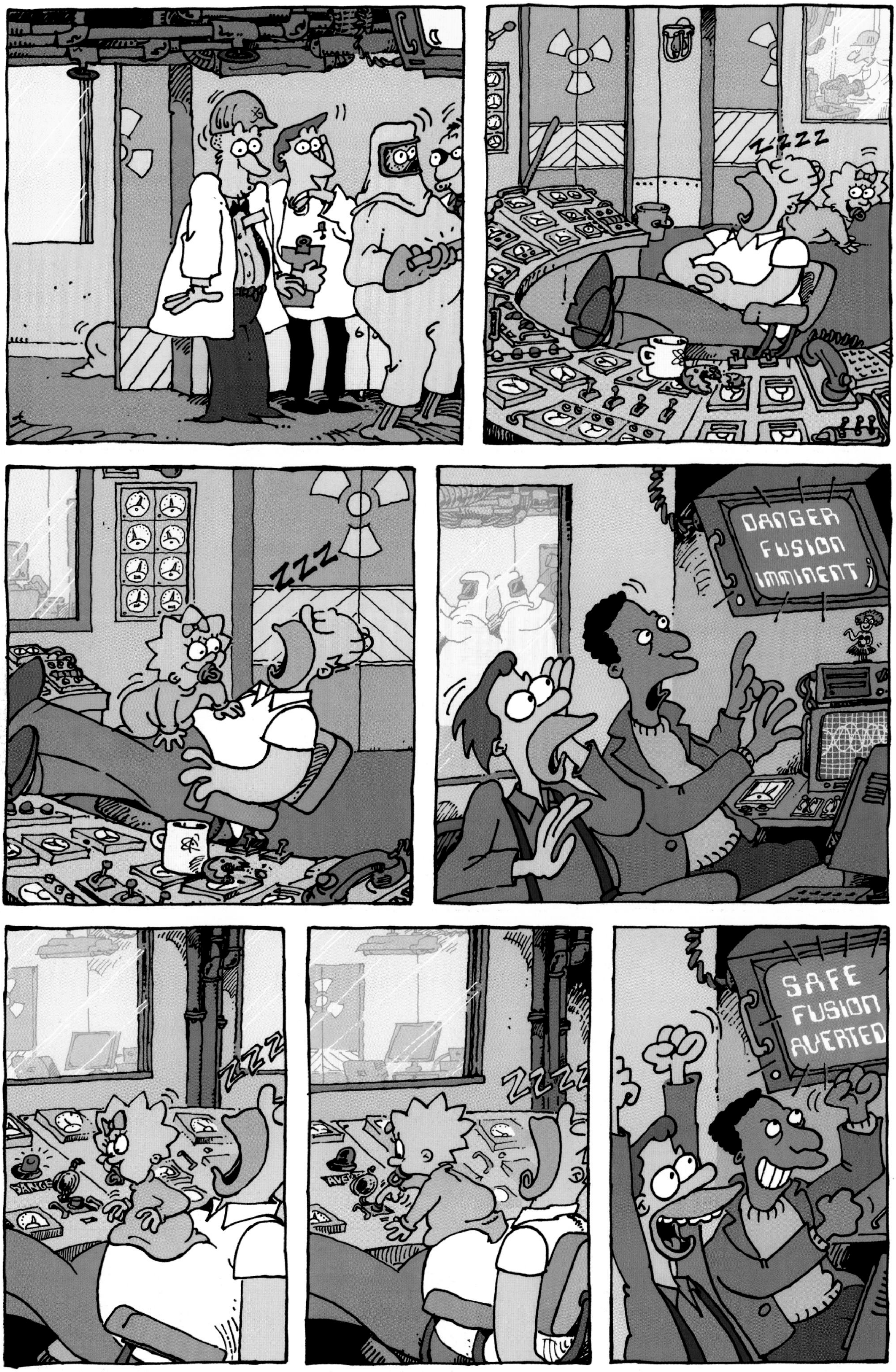
ZZZZ
ZZZ
DANGER
FUSION
IMMINENT
ZZZ
ZZZZ
SAFE
FUSION
AVERTED

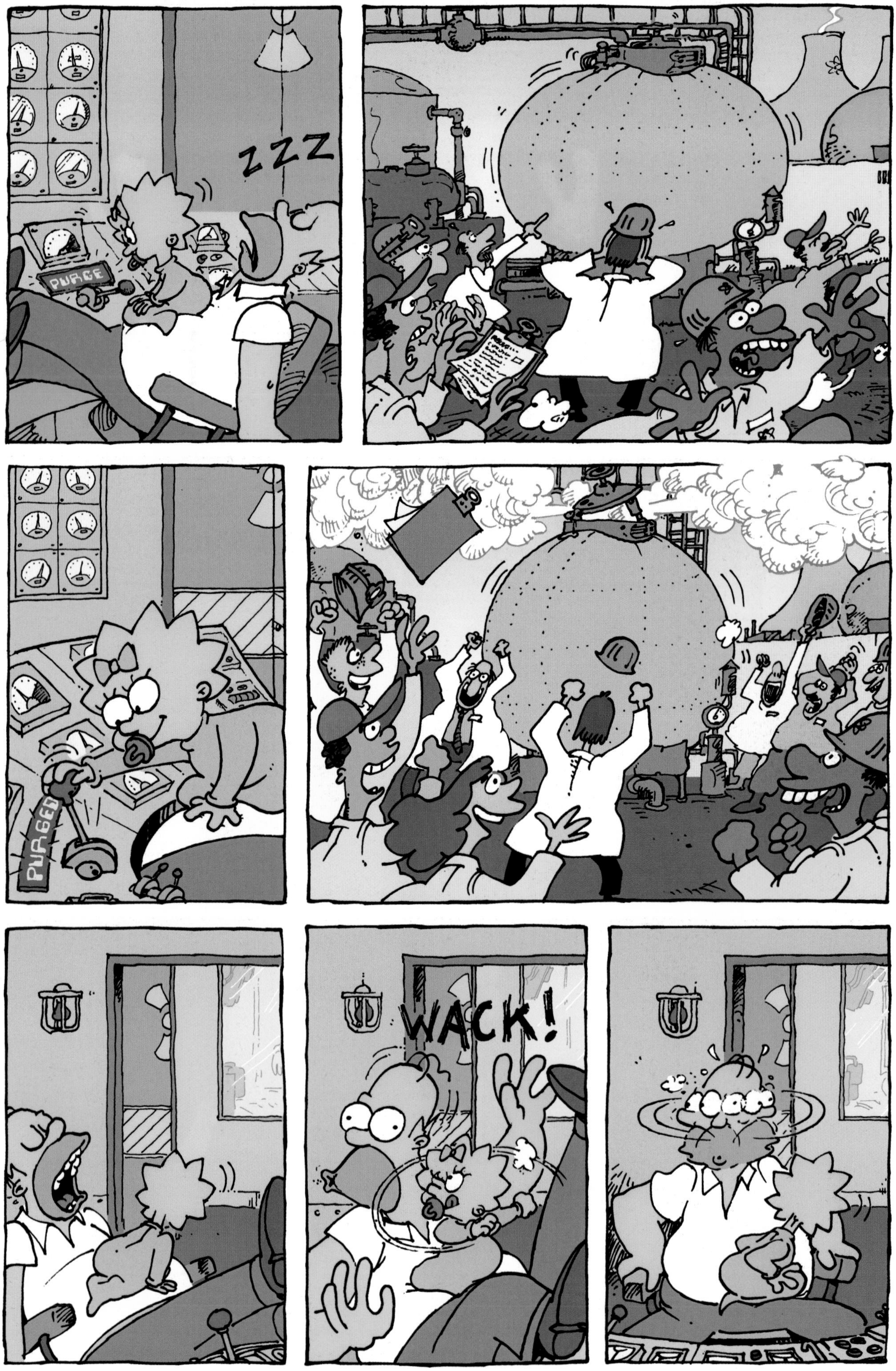
ZZZ
PURGE
PURGED
WACK!

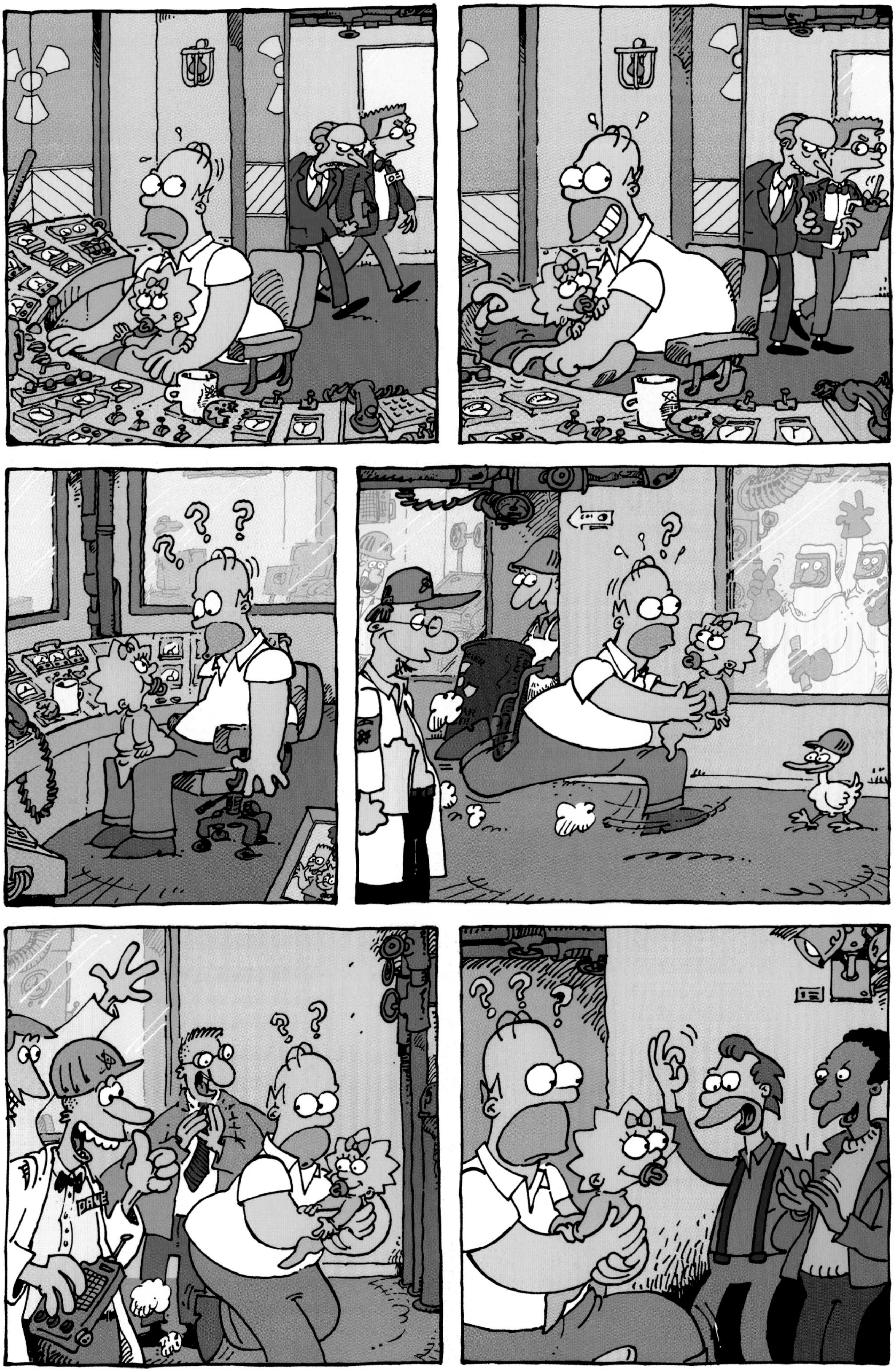
DAVE

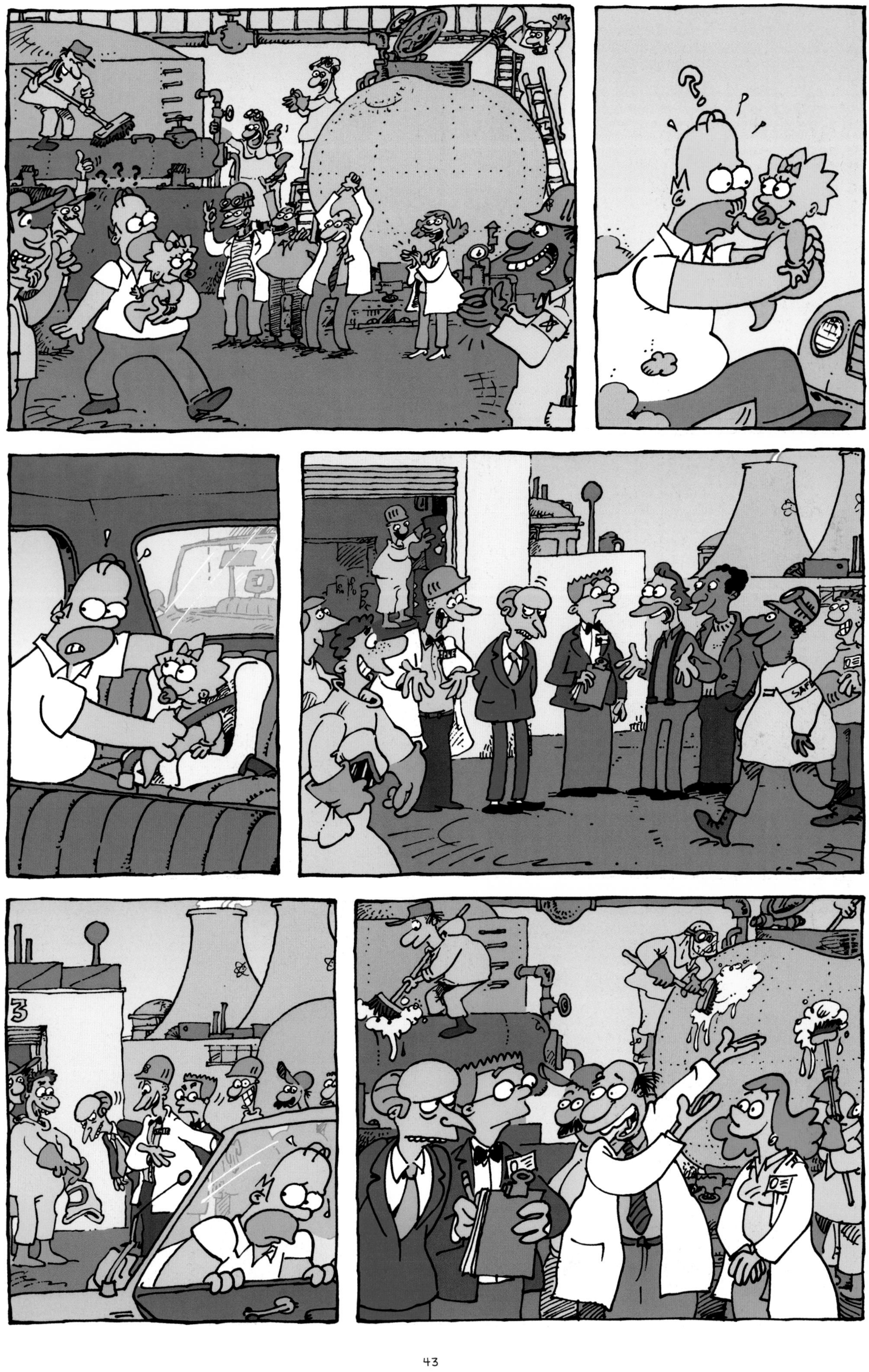

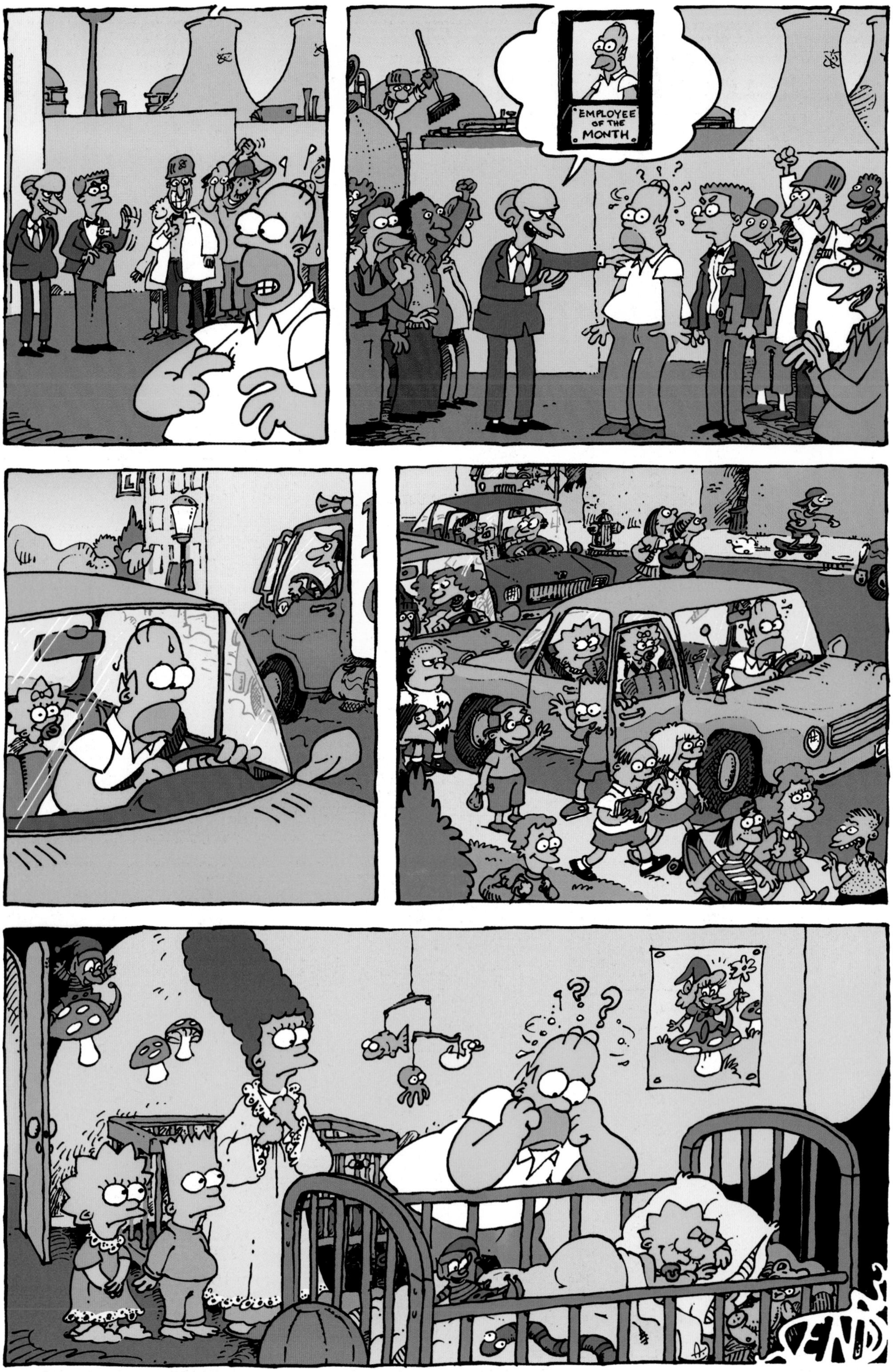
EMPLOYEE OF THE MONTH
END

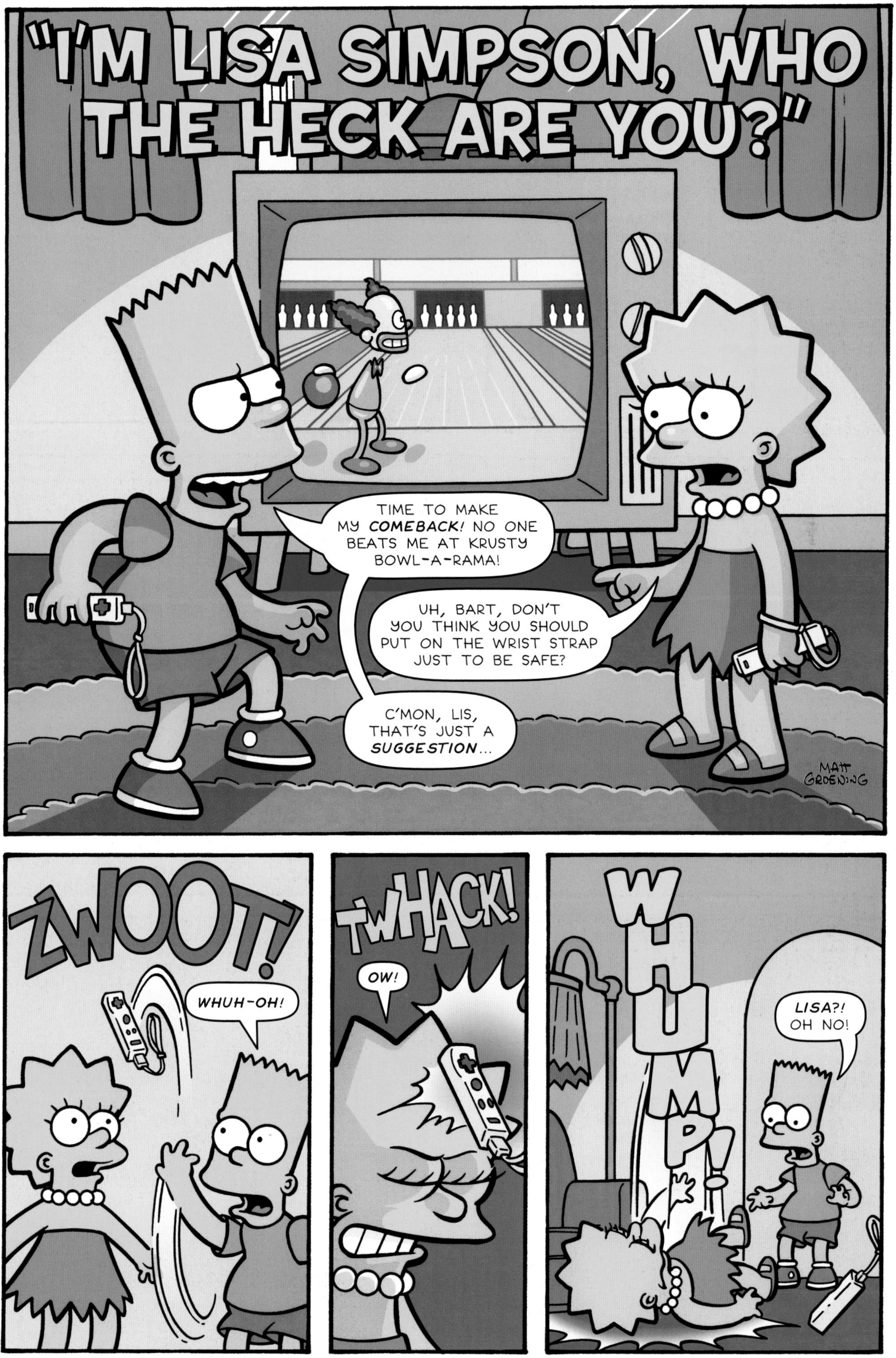
"I'M LISA SIMPSON, WHO THE HECK ARE YOU?"
TIME TO MAKE MY COMEBACK! NO ONE BEATS ME AT KRUSTY BOWL-A-RAMA!
UH, BART, DON'T YOU THINK YOU SHOULD PUT ON THE WRIST STRAP JUST TO BE SAFE?
C'MON, LIS, THAT'S JUST A SUGGESTION...
MATT GROENING
ZWOOT!
WHUH-OH!
TWHACK!
OW!
WHUMP!
LISA?! OH NO!

ERIC ROGERS SCRIPT | **JAMES LLOYD** PENCILS | **ANDREW PEPOY** INKS | **ART VILLANUEVA** COLORS | **KAREN BATES** LETTERS | **BILL MORRISON** EDITOR

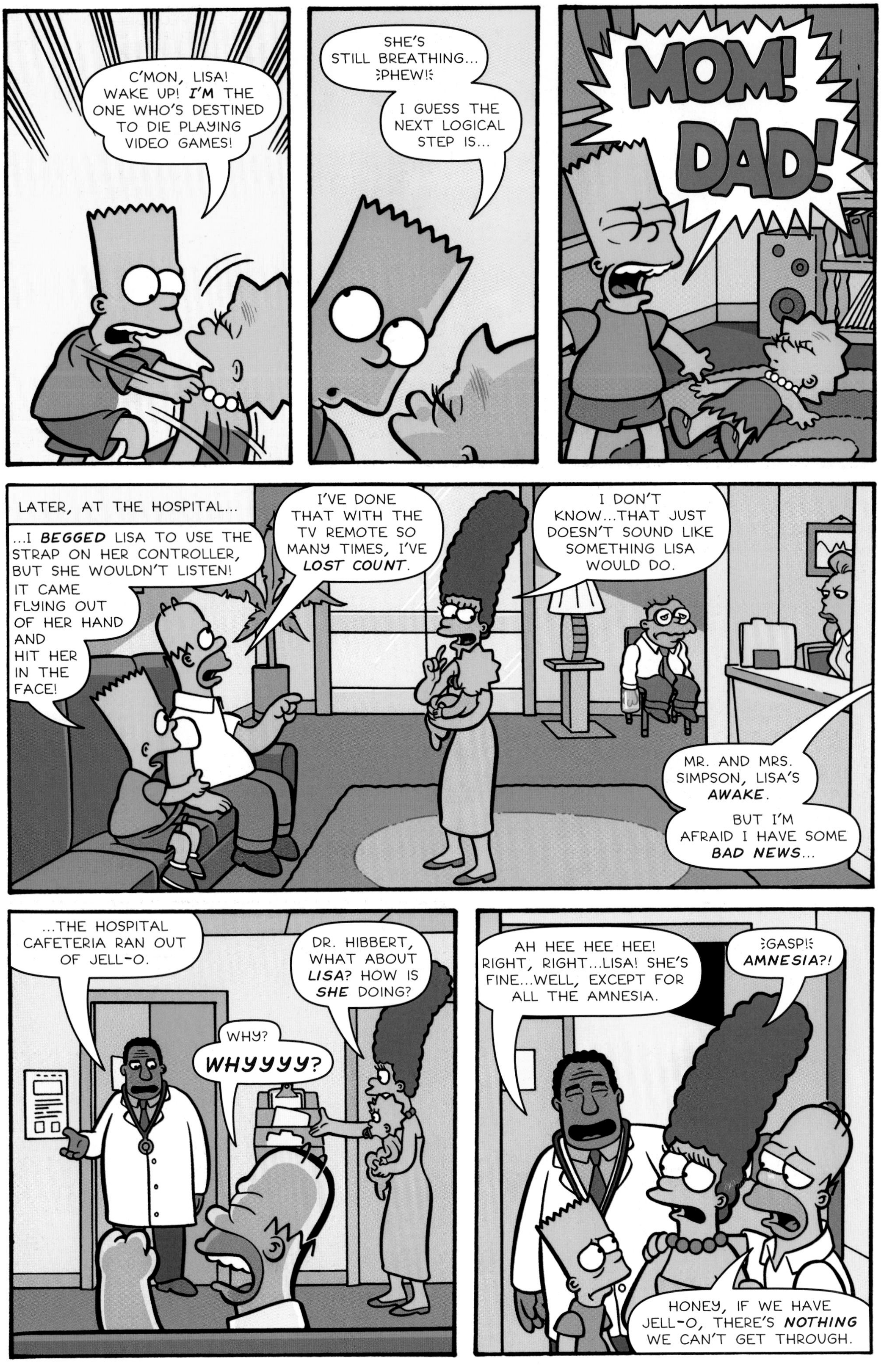
C'MON, LISA! WAKE UP! I'M THE ONE WHO'S DESTINED TO DIE PLAYING VIDEO GAMES!
SHE'S STILL BREATHING... PHEW!
I GUESS THE NEXT LOGICAL STEP IS...
MOM! DAD!
LATER, AT THE HOSPITAL...
...I BEGGED LISA TO USE THE STRAP ON HER CONTROLLER, BUT SHE WOULDN'T LISTEN!
IT CAME FLYING OUT OF HER HAND AND HIT HER IN THE FACE!
I'VE DONE THAT WITH THE TV REMOTE SO MANY TIMES, I'VE LOST COUNT.
I DON'T KNOW...THAT JUST DOESN'T SOUND LIKE SOMETHING LISA WOULD DO.
MR. AND MRS. SIMPSON, LISA'S AWAKE.
BUT I'M AFRAID I HAVE SOME BAD NEWS...
...THE HOSPITAL CAFETERIA RAN OUT OF JELL-O.
WHY? WHYYYY?
DR. HIBBERT, WHAT ABOUT LISA? HOW IS SHE DOING?
AH HEE HEE HEE! RIGHT, RIGHT...LISA! SHE'S FINE...WELL, EXCEPT FOR ALL THE AMNESIA.
GASP! AMNESIA?!
HONEY, IF WE HAVE JELL-O, THERE'S NOTHING WE CAN'T GET THROUGH.

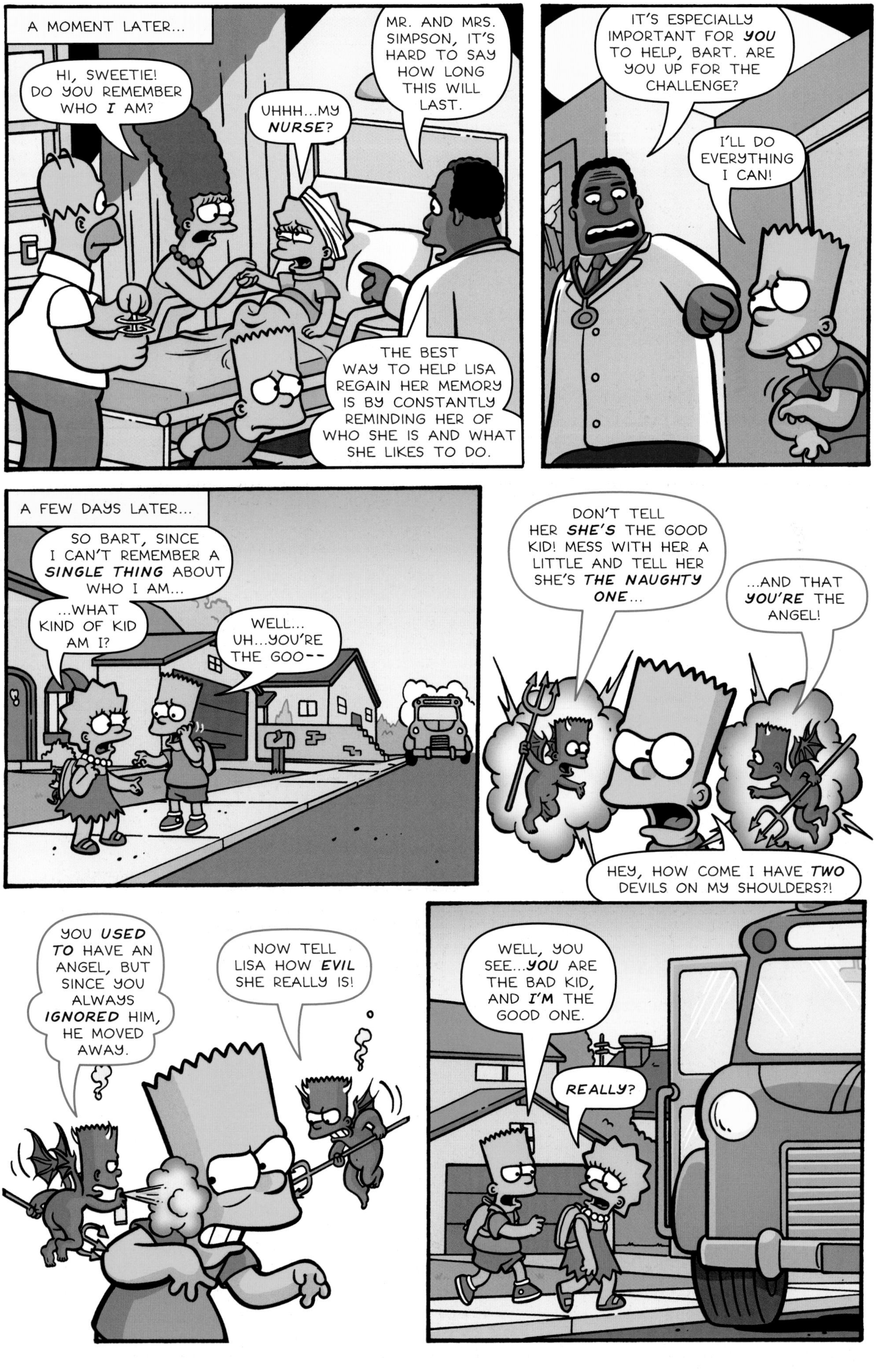

A MOMENT LATER...
HI, SWEETIE! DO YOU REMEMBER WHO I AM?
UHHH...MY NURSE?
MR. AND MRS. SIMPSON, IT'S HARD TO SAY HOW LONG THIS WILL LAST.
THE BEST WAY TO HELP LISA REGAIN HER MEMORY IS BY CONSTANTLY REMINDING HER OF WHO SHE IS AND WHAT SHE LIKES TO DO.
IT'S ESPECIALLY IMPORTANT FOR YOU TO HELP, BART. ARE YOU UP FOR THE CHALLENGE?
I'LL DO EVERYTHING I CAN!
A FEW DAYS LATER...
SO BART, SINCE I CAN'T REMEMBER A SINGLE THING ABOUT WHO I AM...
...WHAT KIND OF KID AM I?
WELL... UH...YOU'RE THE GOO--
DON'T TELL HER SHE'S THE GOOD KID! MESS WITH HER A LITTLE AND TELL HER SHE'S THE NAUGHTY ONE...
...AND THAT YOU'RE THE ANGEL!
HEY, HOW COME I HAVE TWO DEVILS ON MY SHOULDERS?!
YOU USED TO HAVE AN ANGEL, BUT SINCE YOU ALWAYS IGNORED HIM, HE MOVED AWAY.
NOW TELL LISA HOW EVIL SHE REALLY IS!
WELL, YOU SEE...YOU ARE THE BAD KID, AND I'M THE GOOD ONE.
REALLY?

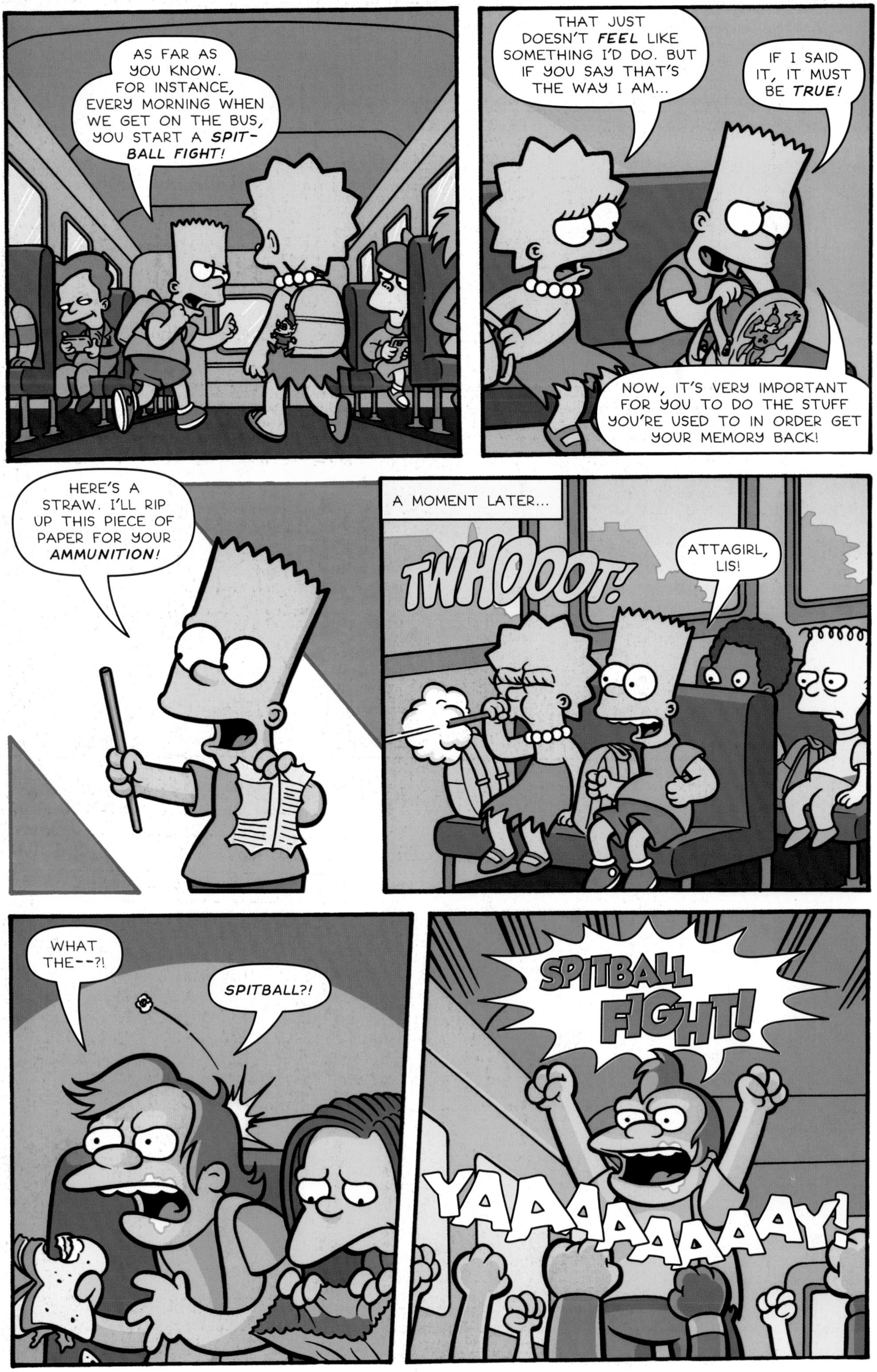
AS FAR AS YOU KNOW. FOR INSTANCE, EVERY MORNING WHEN WE GET ON THE BUS, YOU START A SPIT-BALL FIGHT!
THAT JUST DOESN'T FEEL LIKE SOMETHING I'D DO. BUT IF YOU SAY THAT'S THE WAY I AM...
IF I SAID IT, IT MUST BE TRUE!
NOW, IT'S VERY IMPORTANT FOR YOU TO DO THE STUFF YOU'RE USED TO IN ORDER GET YOUR MEMORY BACK!
HERE'S A STRAW. I'LL RIP UP THIS PIECE OF PAPER FOR YOUR AMMUNITION!
A MOMENT LATER...
TWHOOOT!
ATTAGIRL, LIS!
WHAT THE--?!
SPITBALL?!
SPITBALL FIGHT!
YAAAAAAAAAY!

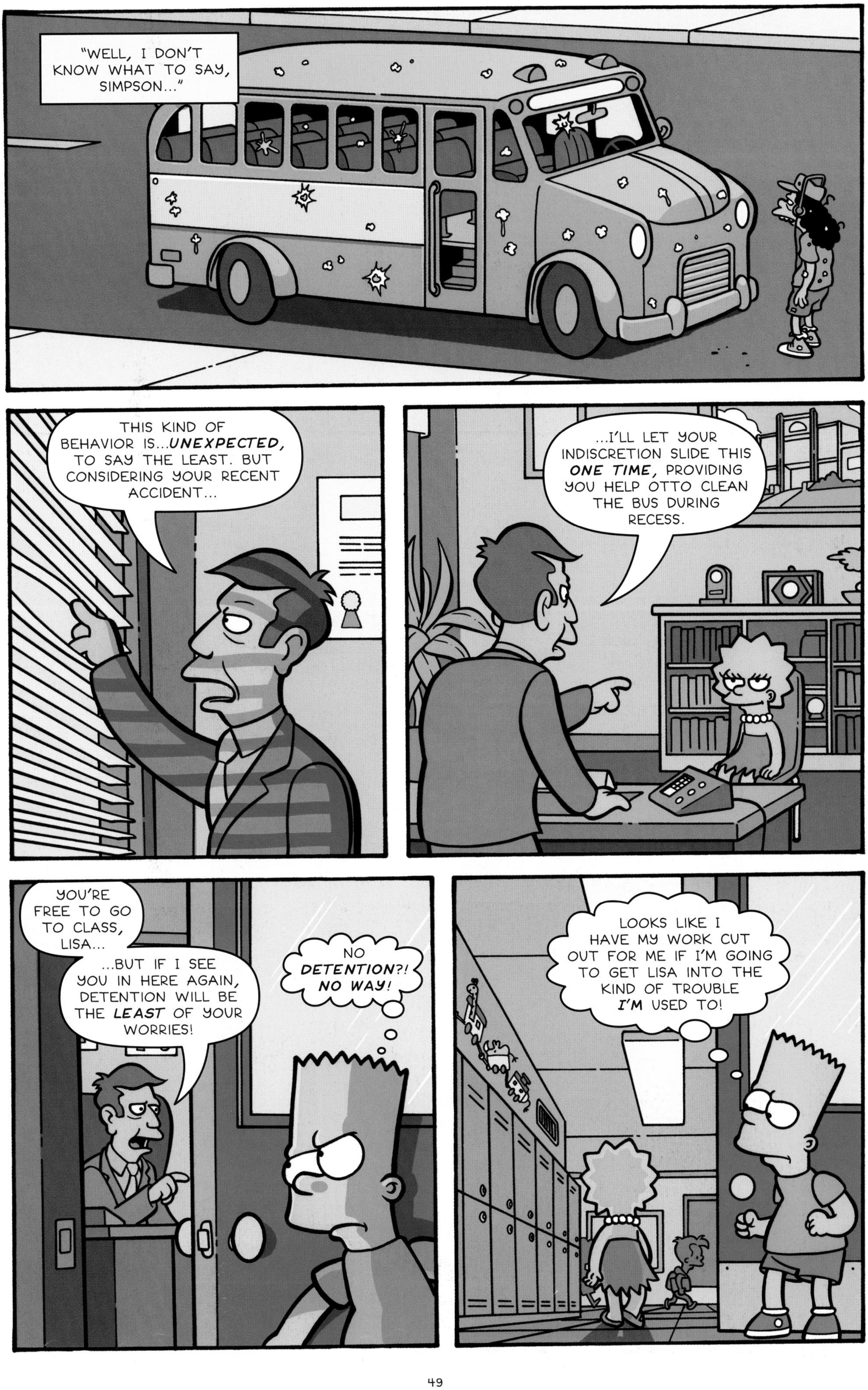

"WELL, I DON'T KNOW WHAT TO SAY, SIMPSON..."
THIS KIND OF BEHAVIOR IS...UNEXPECTED, TO SAY THE LEAST. BUT CONSIDERING YOUR RECENT ACCIDENT...
...I'LL LET YOUR INDISCRETION SLIDE THIS ONE TIME, PROVIDING YOU HELP OTTO CLEAN THE BUS DURING RECESS.
YOU'RE FREE TO GO TO CLASS, LISA...
...BUT IF I SEE YOU IN HERE AGAIN, DETENTION WILL BE THE LEAST OF YOUR WORRIES!
NO DETENTION?! NO WAY!
LOOKS LIKE I HAVE MY WORK CUT OUT FOR ME IF I'M GOING TO GET LISA INTO THE KIND OF TROUBLE I'M USED TO!

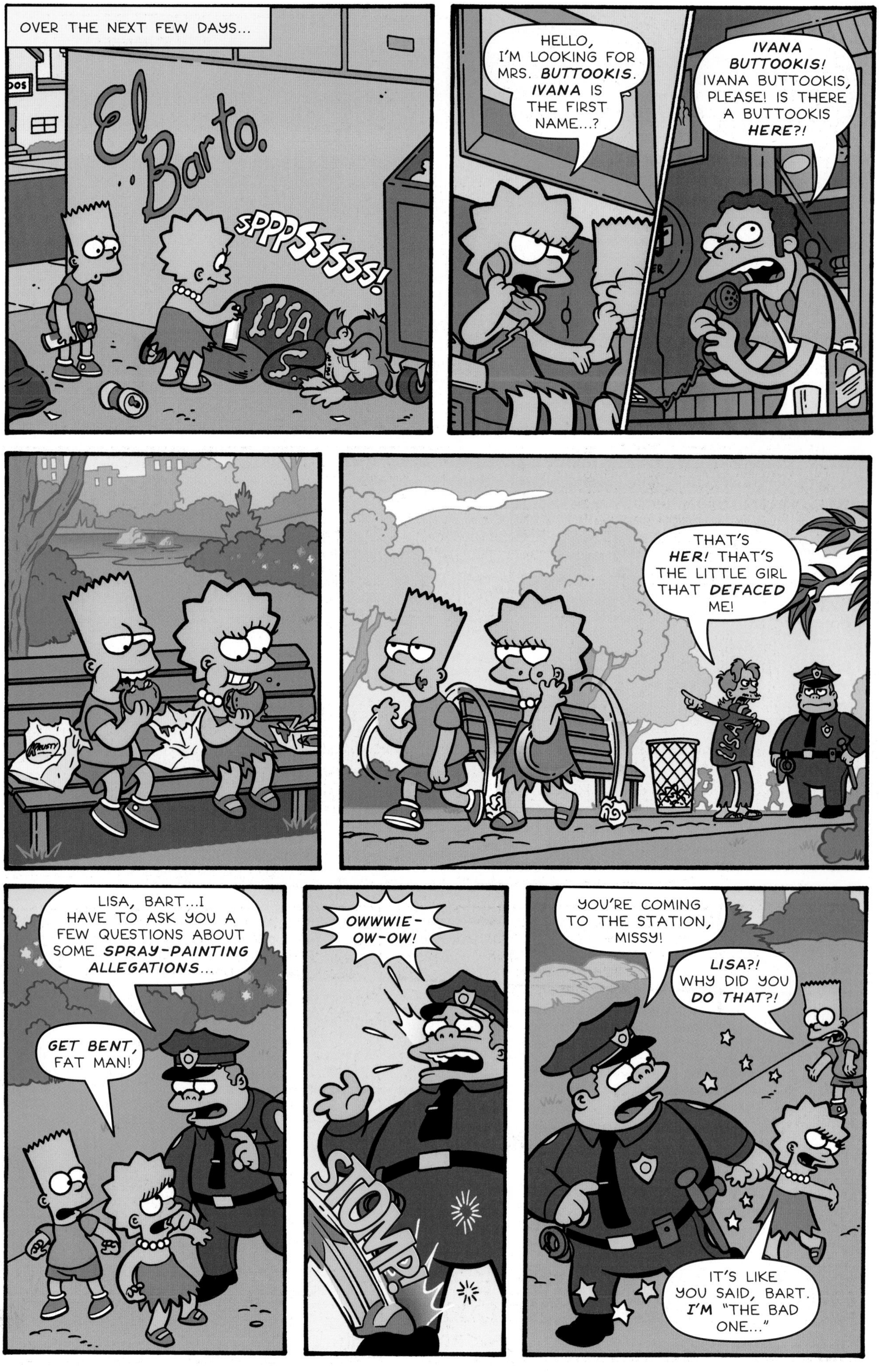

OVER THE NEXT FEW DAYS...
El Barto.
SPPPSSSSS!
LISA S.
HELLO, I'M LOOKING FOR MRS. BUTTOOKIS. IVANA IS THE FIRST NAME...?
IVANA BUTTOOKIS! IVANA BUTTOOKIS, PLEASE! IS THERE A BUTTOOKIS HERE?!
THAT'S HER! THAT'S THE LITTLE GIRL THAT DEFACED ME!
LISA, BART...I HAVE TO ASK YOU A FEW QUESTIONS ABOUT SOME SPRAY-PAINTING ALLEGATIONS...
GET BENT, FAT MAN!
OWWWIE-OW-OW!
STOMP!
YOU'RE COMING TO THE STATION, MISSY!
LISA?! WHY DID YOU DO THAT?!
IT'S LIKE YOU SAID, BART. I'M "THE BAD ONE..."

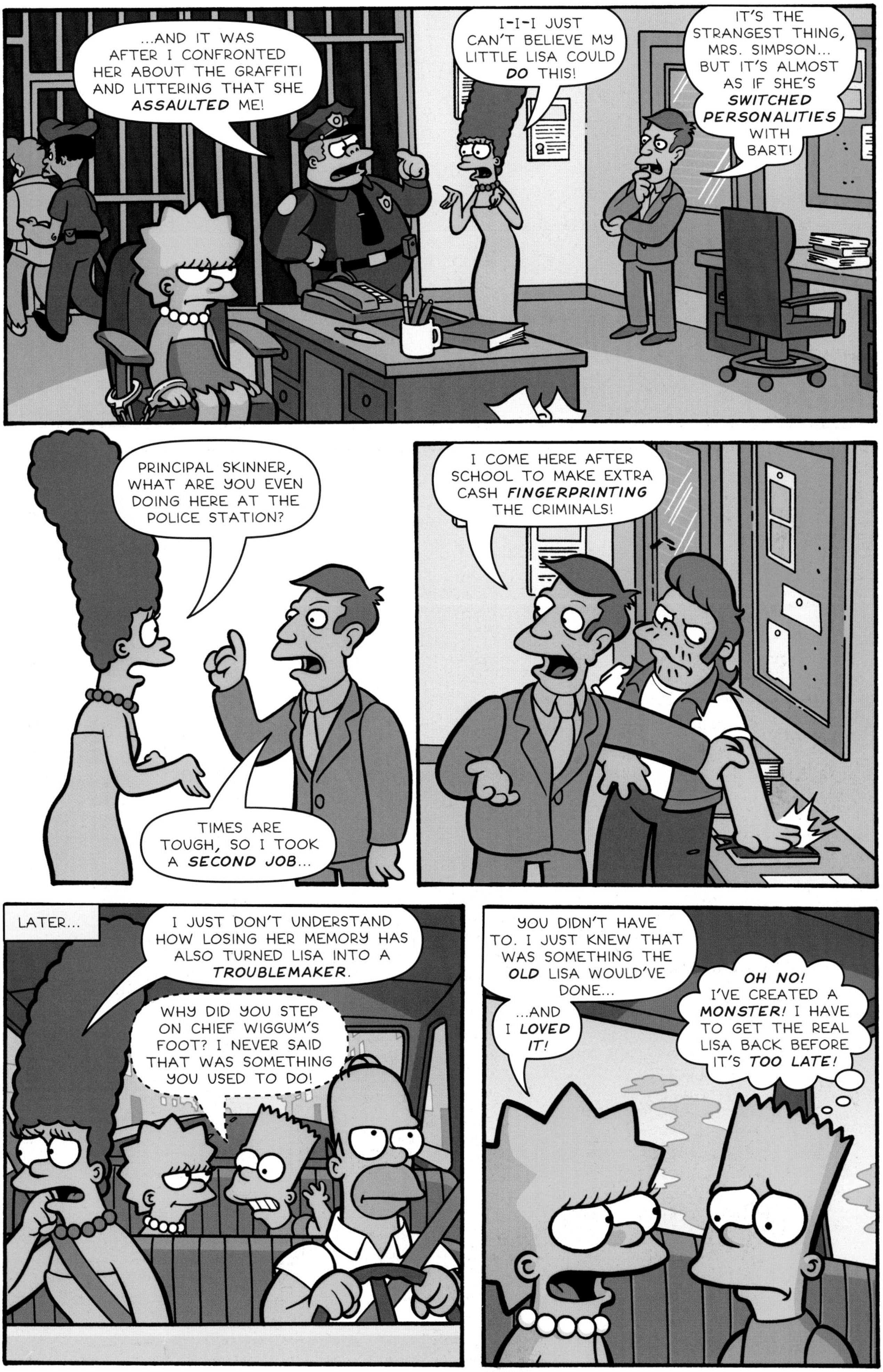
...AND IT WAS AFTER I CONFRONTED HER ABOUT THE GRAFFITI AND LITTERING THAT SHE ASSAULTED ME!
I-I-I JUST CAN'T BELIEVE MY LITTLE LISA COULD DO THIS!
IT'S THE STRANGEST THING, MRS. SIMPSON... BUT IT'S ALMOST AS IF SHE'S SWITCHED PERSONALITIES WITH BART!
PRINCIPAL SKINNER, WHAT ARE YOU EVEN DOING HERE AT THE POLICE STATION?
TIMES ARE TOUGH, SO I TOOK A SECOND JOB...
I COME HERE AFTER SCHOOL TO MAKE EXTRA CASH FINGERPRINTING THE CRIMINALS!
LATER...
I JUST DON'T UNDERSTAND HOW LOSING HER MEMORY HAS ALSO TURNED LISA INTO A TROUBLEMAKER.
WHY DID YOU STEP ON CHIEF WIGGUM'S FOOT? I NEVER SAID THAT WAS SOMETHING YOU USED TO DO!
YOU DIDN'T HAVE TO. I JUST KNEW THAT WAS SOMETHING THE OLD LISA WOULD'VE DONE...
...AND I LOVED IT!
OH NO! I'VE CREATED A MONSTER! I HAVE TO GET THE REAL LISA BACK BEFORE IT'S TOO LATE!

A FEW MINUTES LATER...

GO STRAIGHT TO YOUR ROOM, LISA! YOU'RE *GROUNDED*!

CRUD, I HAVE TO ACT FAST!

HEY, LIS, HOW 'BOUT A QUICK GAME OF KRUSTY BOWLING IN MY ROOM BEFORE YOUR GROUNDING BEGINS?

SOUNDS GOOD TO ME!

THE OLD LISA WOULD DEFINITELY *DEFY* MOM AND DAD *ONE LAST TIME*!

A MOMENT LATER...

COME ON, BART, WE DON'T HAVE *ALL DAY*!

JUST MAKING SURE YOU'RE IN THE *RIGHT SPOT*...

EL BARTO   STRIKEGIRL

FOR *WHAT*?!

FOR *THIS*!

AGCK!

TWHACK!

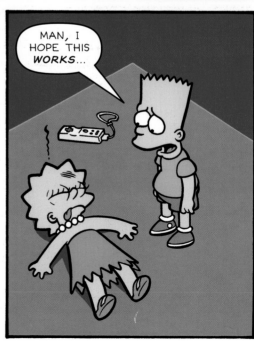

MAN, I HOPE THIS *WORKS*...

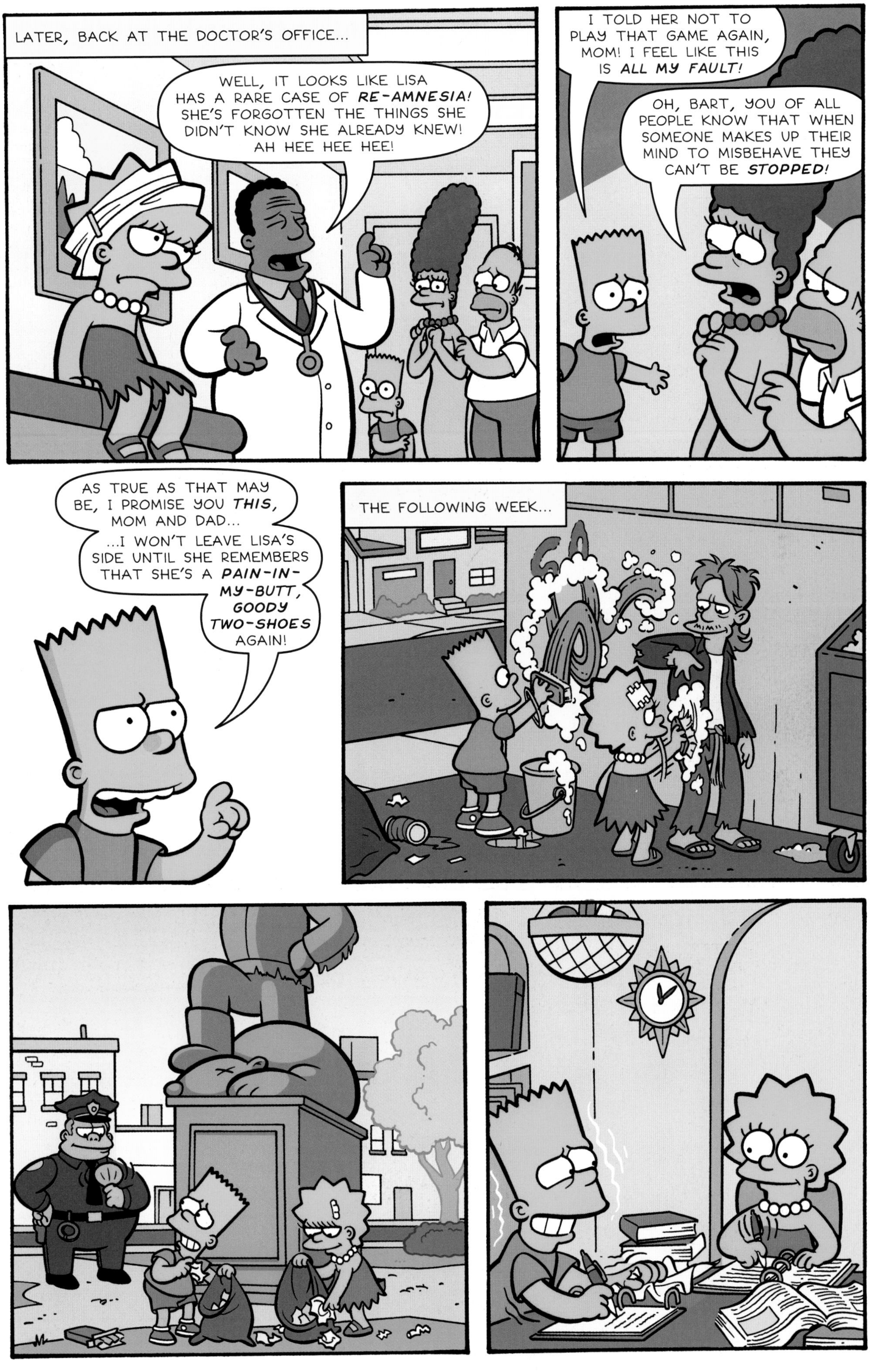
LATER, BACK AT THE DOCTOR'S OFFICE...
WELL, IT LOOKS LIKE LISA HAS A RARE CASE OF RE-AMNESIA! SHE'S FORGOTTEN THE THINGS SHE DIDN'T KNOW SHE ALREADY KNEW! AH HEE HEE HEE!
I TOLD HER NOT TO PLAY THAT GAME AGAIN, MOM! I FEEL LIKE THIS IS ALL MY FAULT!
OH, BART, YOU OF ALL PEOPLE KNOW THAT WHEN SOMEONE MAKES UP THEIR MIND TO MISBEHAVE THEY CAN'T BE STOPPED!
AS TRUE AS THAT MAY BE, I PROMISE YOU THIS, MOM AND DAD...
...I WON'T LEAVE LISA'S SIDE UNTIL SHE REMEMBERS THAT SHE'S A PAIN-IN-MY-BUTT, GOODY TWO-SHOES AGAIN!
THE FOLLOWING WEEK...

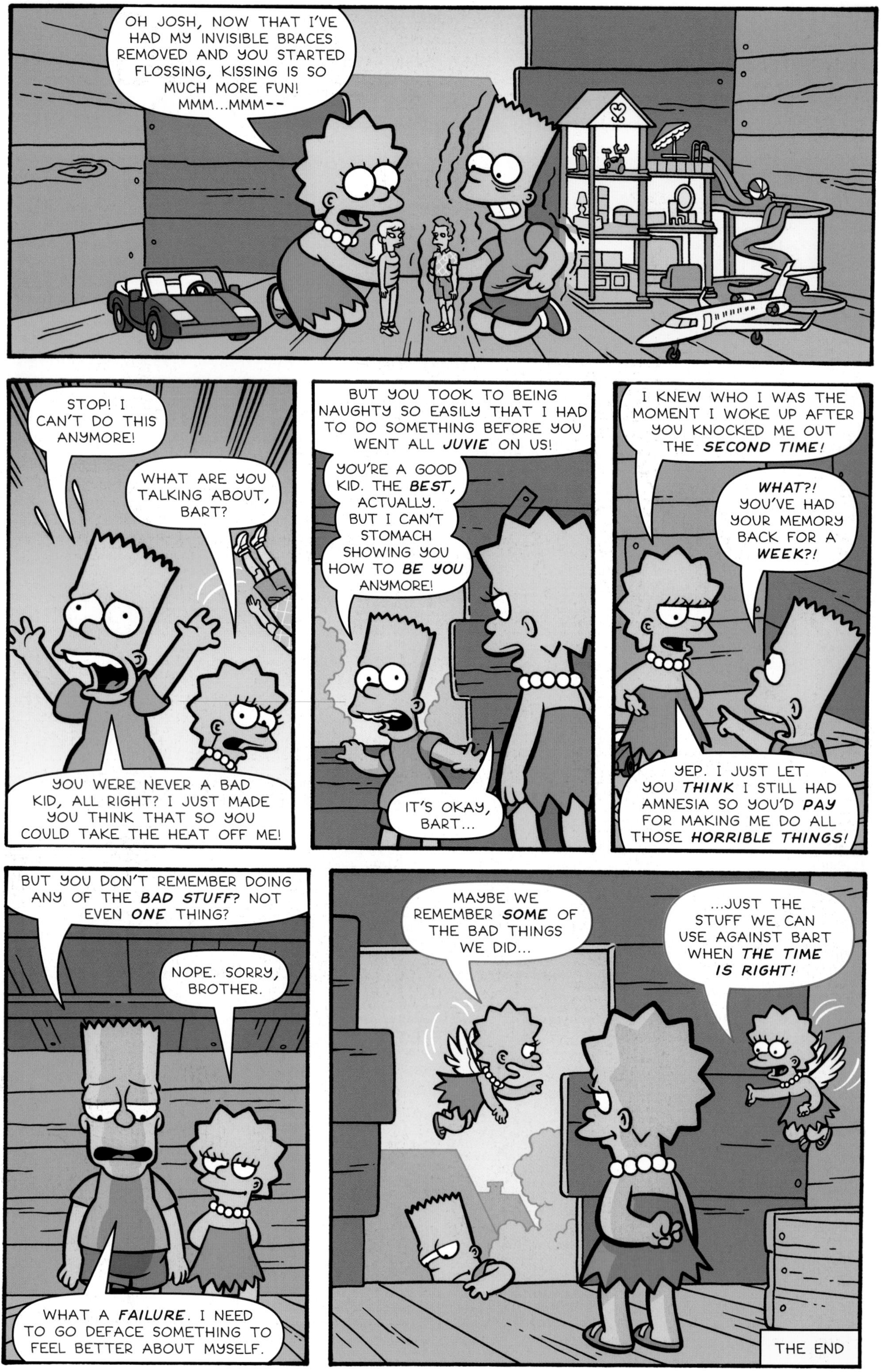
OH JOSH, NOW THAT I'VE HAD MY INVISIBLE BRACES REMOVED AND YOU STARTED FLOSSING, KISSING IS SO MUCH MORE FUN! MMM...MMM--
STOP! I CAN'T DO THIS ANYMORE!
WHAT ARE YOU TALKING ABOUT, BART?
YOU WERE NEVER A BAD KID, ALL RIGHT? I JUST MADE YOU THINK THAT SO YOU COULD TAKE THE HEAT OFF ME!
BUT YOU TOOK TO BEING NAUGHTY SO EASILY THAT I HAD TO DO SOMETHING BEFORE YOU WENT ALL *JUVIE* ON US!
YOU'RE A GOOD KID. THE *BEST*, ACTUALLY. BUT I CAN'T STOMACH SHOWING YOU HOW TO *BE YOU* ANYMORE!
IT'S OKAY, BART...
I KNEW WHO I WAS THE MOMENT I WOKE UP AFTER YOU KNOCKED ME OUT THE *SECOND TIME*!
WHAT?! YOU'VE HAD YOUR MEMORY BACK FOR A *WEEK*?!
YEP. I JUST LET YOU *THINK* I STILL HAD AMNESIA SO YOU'D *PAY* FOR MAKING ME DO ALL THOSE *HORRIBLE THINGS*!
BUT YOU DON'T REMEMBER DOING ANY OF THE *BAD STUFF*? NOT EVEN *ONE* THING?
NOPE. SORRY, BROTHER.
WHAT A *FAILURE*. I NEED TO GO DEFACE SOMETHING TO FEEL BETTER ABOUT MYSELF.
MAYBE WE REMEMBER *SOME* OF THE BAD THINGS WE DID...
...JUST THE STUFF WE CAN USE AGAINST BART WHEN *THE TIME IS RIGHT*!
THE END

BART SIMPSON: WARLORD

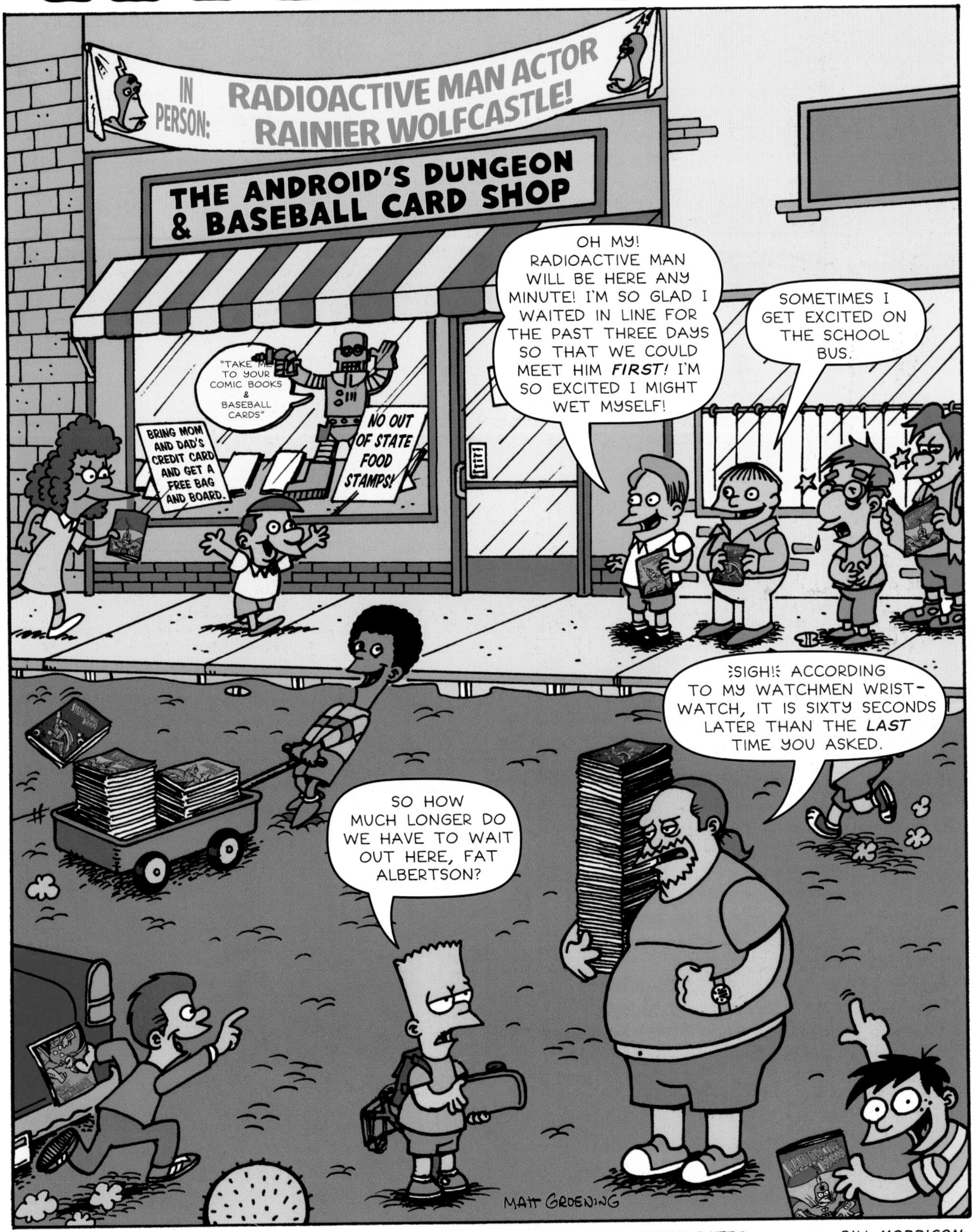

IN PERSON: RADIOACTIVE MAN ACTOR RAINIER WOLFCASTLE!
THE ANDROID'S DUNGEON & BASEBALL CARD SHOP
"TAKE ME TO YOUR COMIC BOOKS & BASEBALL CARDS"
BRING MOM AND DAD'S CREDIT CARD AND GET A FREE BAG AND BOARD.
NO OUT OF STATE FOOD STAMPS!
OH MY! RADIOACTIVE MAN WILL BE HERE ANY MINUTE! I'M SO GLAD I WAITED IN LINE FOR THE PAST THREE DAYS SO THAT WE COULD MEET HIM FIRST! I'M SO EXCITED I MIGHT WET MYSELF!
SOMETIMES I GET EXCITED ON THE SCHOOL BUS.
SO HOW MUCH LONGER DO WE HAVE TO WAIT OUT HERE, FAT ALBERTSON?
:SIGH!: ACCORDING TO MY WATCHMEN WRIST-WATCH, IT IS SIXTY SECONDS LATER THAN THE LAST TIME YOU ASKED.
MATT GROENING

CHRIS YAMBAR SCRIPT | SCOTT SHAW! PENCILS & INKS | NATHAN HAMILL COLORS | KAREN BATES LETTERS | BILL MORRISON EDITOR

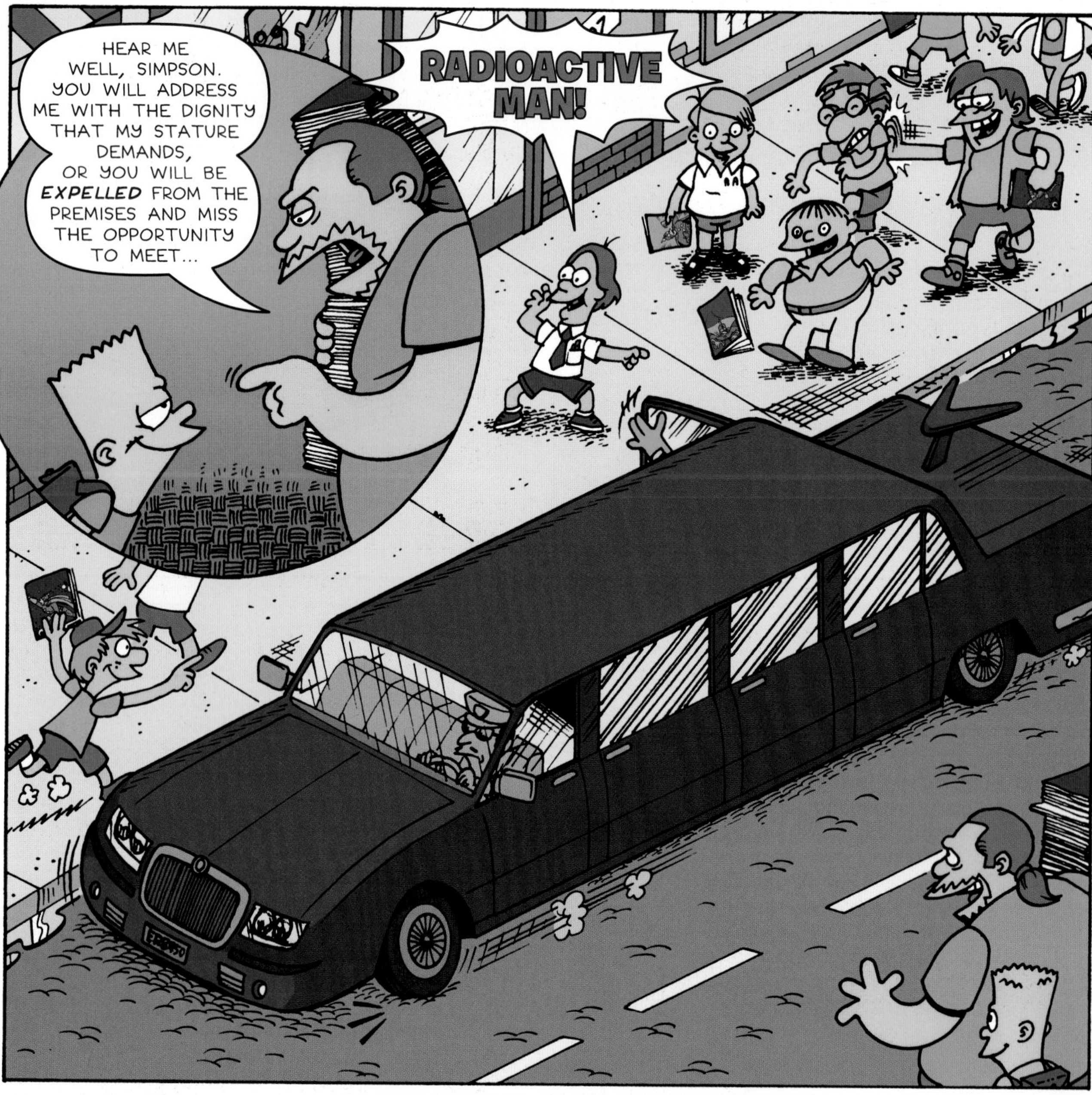
HEAR ME WELL, SIMPSON. YOU WILL ADDRESS ME WITH THE DIGNITY THAT MY STATURE DEMANDS, OR YOU WILL BE *EXPELLED* FROM THE PREMISES AND MISS THE OPPORTUNITY TO MEET...
RADIOACTIVE MAN!

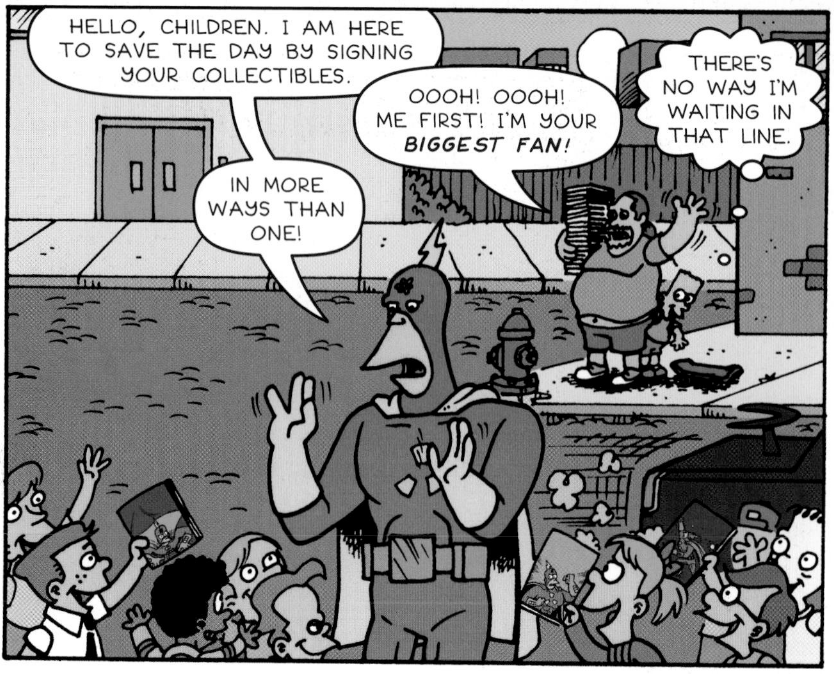
HELLO, CHILDREN. I AM HERE TO SAVE THE DAY BY SIGNING YOUR COLLECTIBLES.
IN MORE WAYS THAN ONE!
OOOH! OOOH! ME FIRST! I'M YOUR *BIGGEST FAN!*
THERE'S NO WAY I'M WAITING IN THAT LINE.

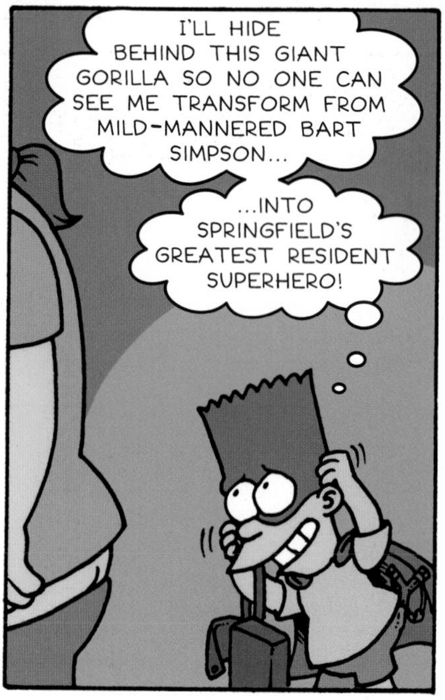
I'LL HIDE BEHIND THIS GIANT GORILLA SO NO ONE CAN SEE ME TRANSFORM FROM MILD-MANNERED BART SIMPSON...
...INTO SPRINGFIELD'S GREATEST RESIDENT SUPERHERO!

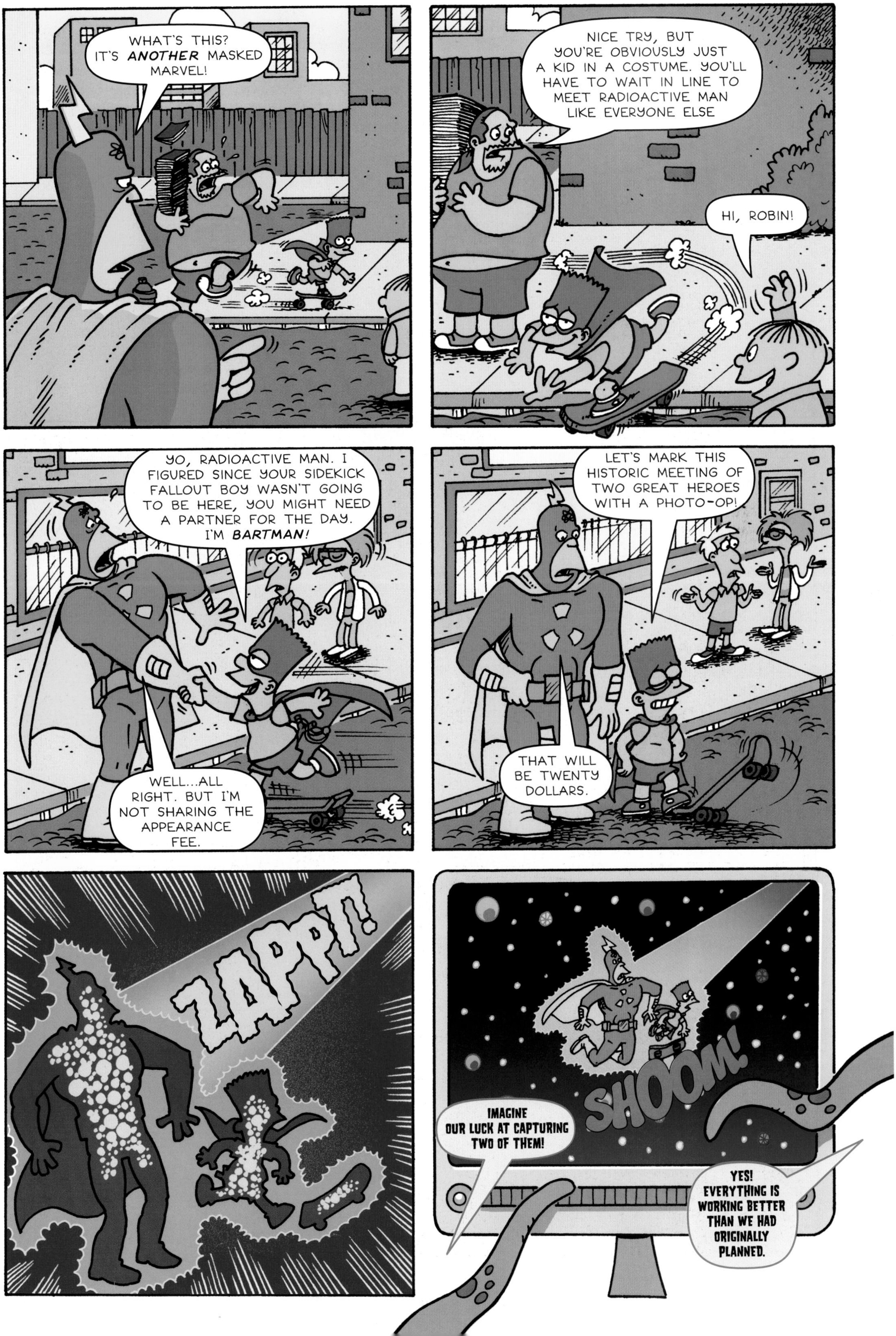
WHAT'S THIS? IT'S ANOTHER MASKED MARVEL!
NICE TRY, BUT YOU'RE OBVIOUSLY JUST A KID IN A COSTUME. YOU'LL HAVE TO WAIT IN LINE TO MEET RADIOACTIVE MAN LIKE EVERYONE ELSE
HI, ROBIN!
YO, RADIOACTIVE MAN. I FIGURED SINCE YOUR SIDEKICK FALLOUT BOY WASN'T GOING TO BE HERE, YOU MIGHT NEED A PARTNER FOR THE DAY. I'M BARTMAN!
WELL...ALL RIGHT. BUT I'M NOT SHARING THE APPEARANCE FEE.
LET'S MARK THIS HISTORIC MEETING OF TWO GREAT HEROES WITH A PHOTO-OP!
THAT WILL BE TWENTY DOLLARS.
ZAPPT!
SHOOM!
IMAGINE OUR LUCK AT CAPTURING TWO OF THEM!
YES! EVERYTHING IS WORKING BETTER THAN WE HAD ORIGINALLY PLANNED.

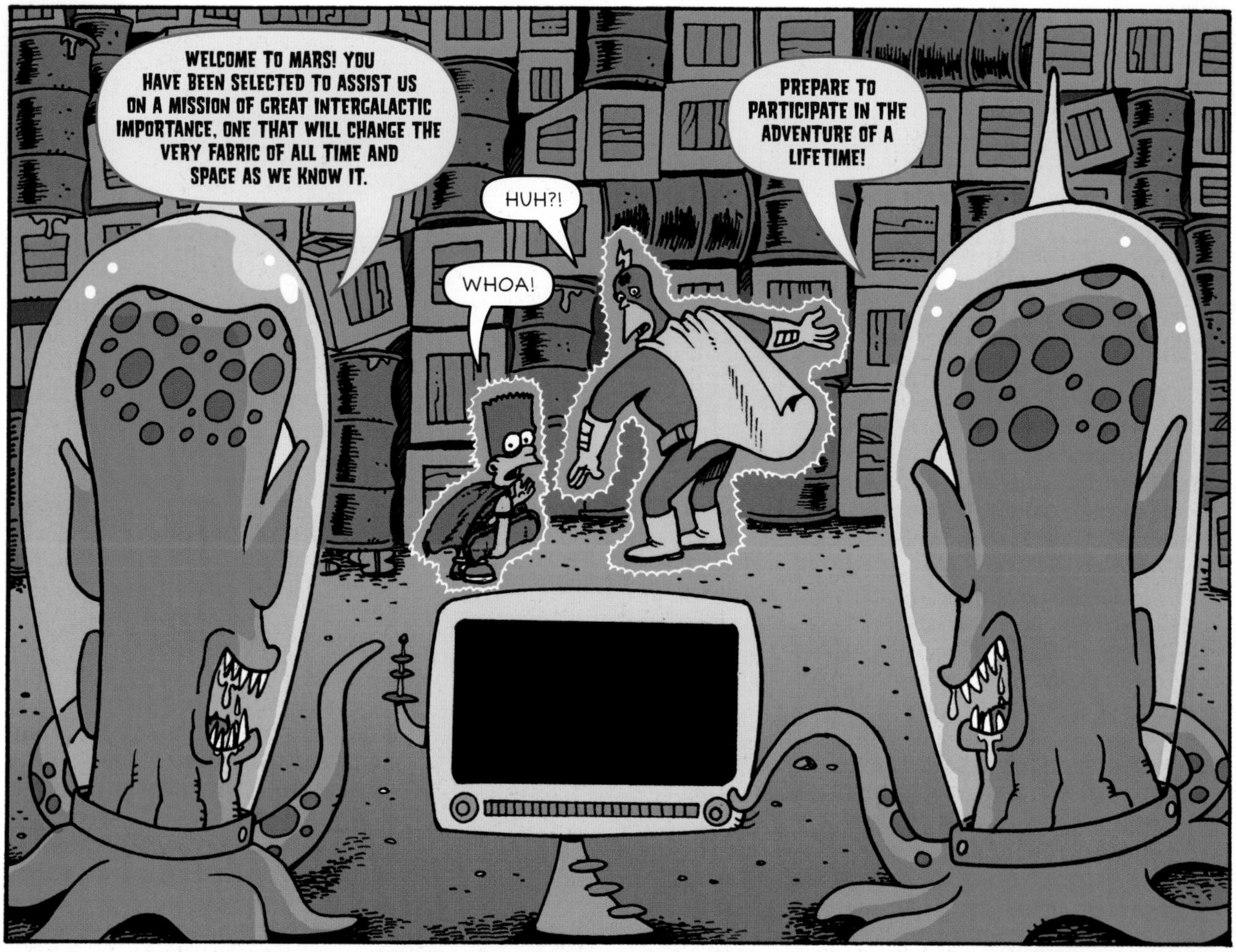
WELCOME TO MARS! YOU HAVE BEEN SELECTED TO ASSIST US ON A MISSION OF GREAT INTERGALACTIC IMPORTANCE, ONE THAT WILL CHANGE THE VERY FABRIC OF ALL TIME AND SPACE AS WE KNOW IT.
HUH?!
WHOA!
PREPARE TO PARTICIPATE IN THE ADVENTURE OF A LIFETIME!

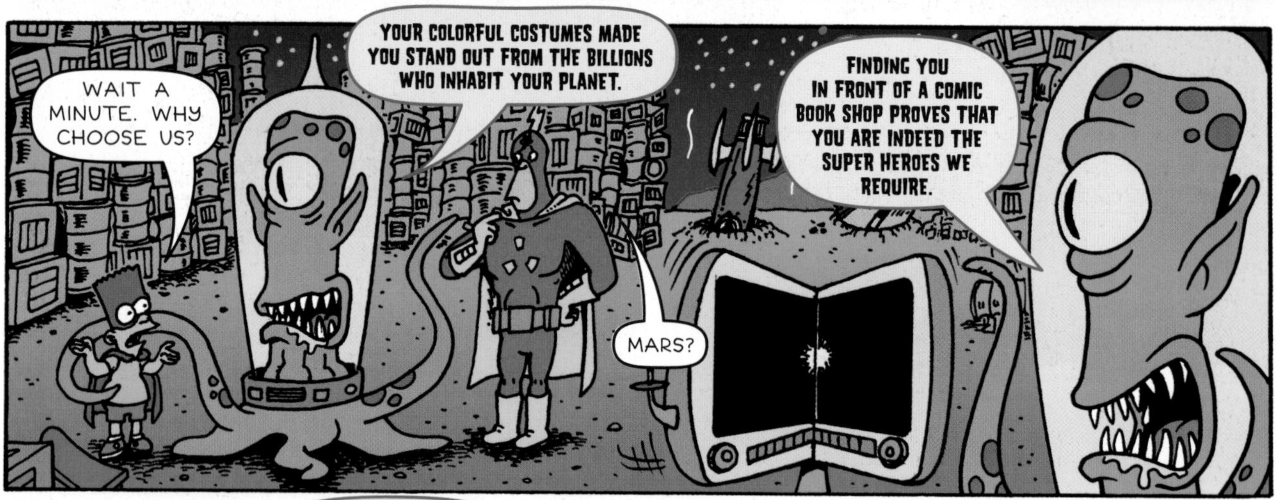
WAIT A MINUTE. WHY CHOOSE US?
YOUR COLORFUL COSTUMES MADE YOU STAND OUT FROM THE BILLIONS WHO INHABIT YOUR PLANET.
MARS?
FINDING YOU IN FRONT OF A COMIC BOOK SHOP PROVES THAT YOU ARE INDEED THE SUPER HEROES WE REQUIRE.

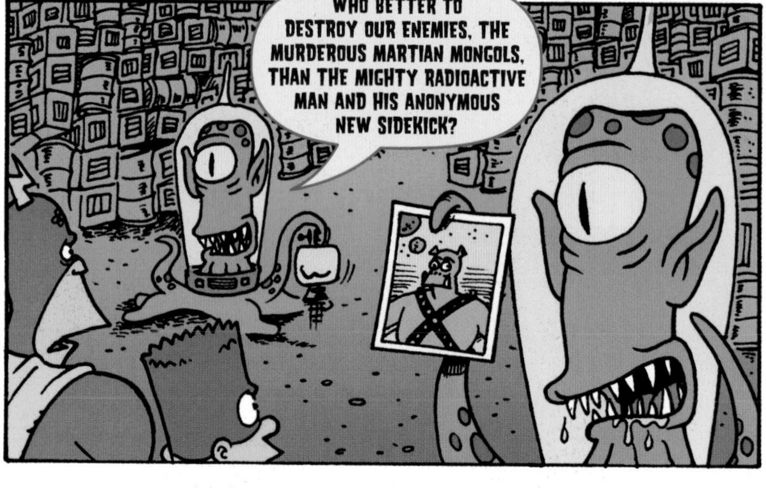
WHO BETTER TO DESTROY OUR ENEMIES, THE MURDEROUS MARTIAN MONGOLS, THAN THE MIGHTY RADIOACTIVE MAN AND HIS ANONYMOUS NEW SIDEKICK?

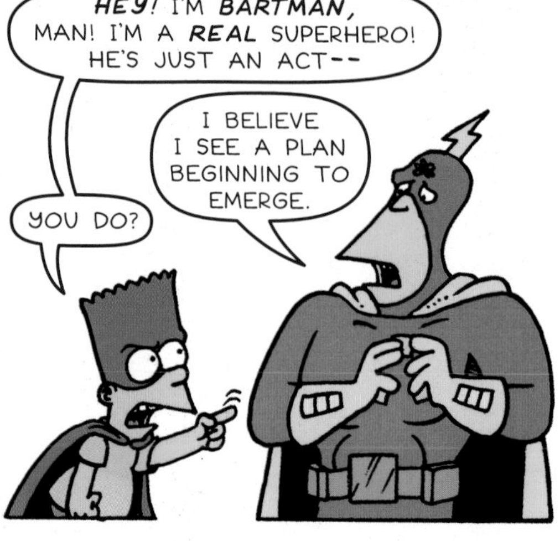
HEY! I'M BARTMAN, MAN! I'M A REAL SUPERHERO! HE'S JUST AN ACT--
I BELIEVE I SEE A PLAN BEGINNING TO EMERGE.
YOU DO?

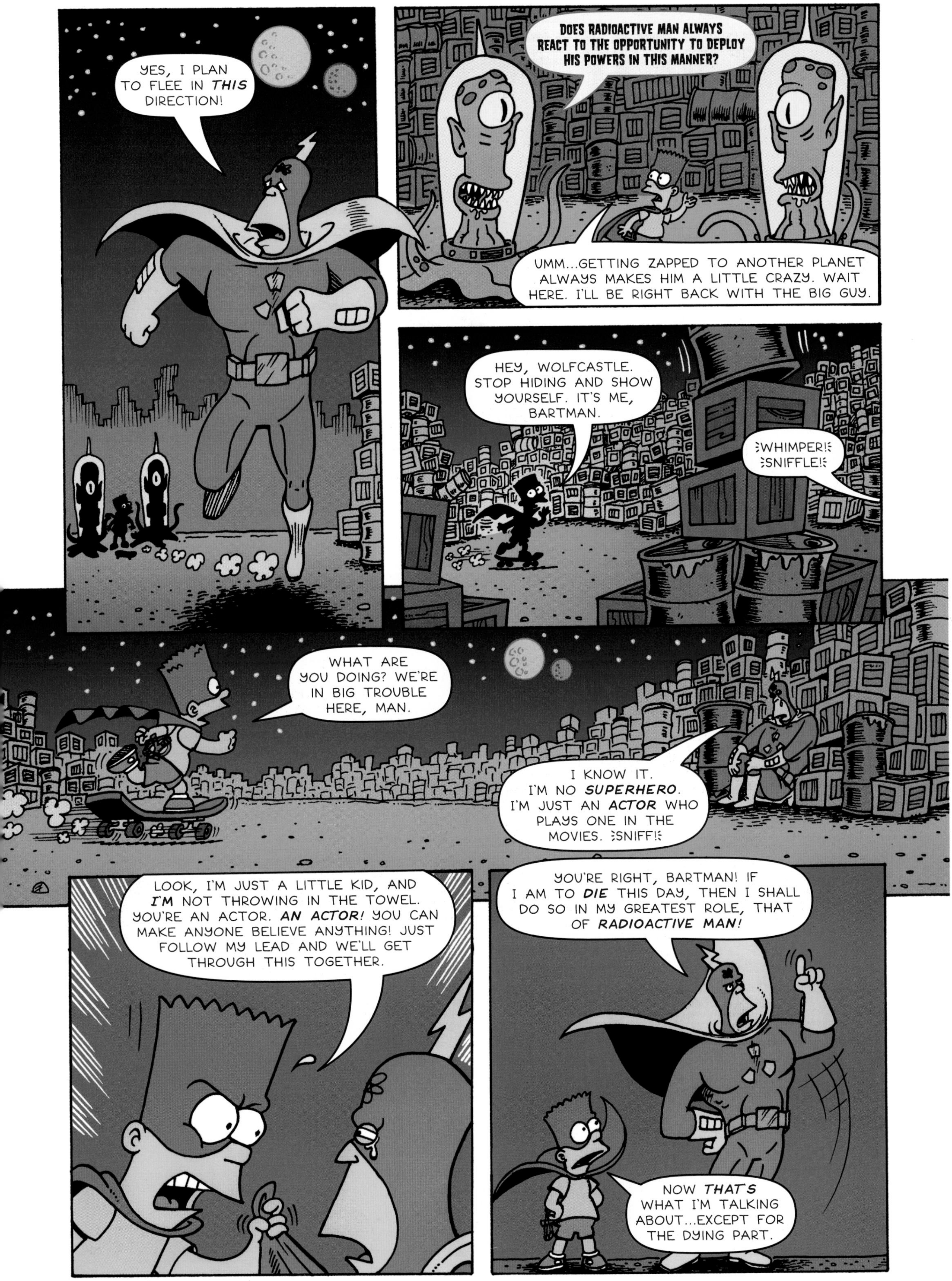
YES, I PLAN TO FLEE IN *THIS* DIRECTION!
DOES RADIOACTIVE MAN ALWAYS REACT TO THE OPPORTUNITY TO DEPLOY HIS POWERS IN THIS MANNER?
UMM...GETTING ZAPPED TO ANOTHER PLANET ALWAYS MAKES HIM A LITTLE CRAZY. WAIT HERE. I'LL BE RIGHT BACK WITH THE BIG GUY.
HEY, WOLFCASTLE. STOP HIDING AND SHOW YOURSELF. IT'S ME, BARTMAN.
WHIMPER! SNIFFLE!
WHAT ARE YOU DOING? WE'RE IN BIG TROUBLE HERE, MAN.
I KNOW IT. I'M NO *SUPERHERO*. I'M JUST AN *ACTOR* WHO PLAYS ONE IN THE MOVIES. SNIFF!
LOOK, I'M JUST A LITTLE KID, AND *I'M* NOT THROWING IN THE TOWEL. YOU'RE AN ACTOR. *AN ACTOR!* YOU CAN MAKE ANYONE BELIEVE ANYTHING! JUST FOLLOW MY LEAD AND WE'LL GET THROUGH THIS TOGETHER.
YOU'RE RIGHT, BARTMAN! IF I AM TO *DIE* THIS DAY, THEN I SHALL DO SO IN MY GREATEST ROLE, THAT OF *RADIOACTIVE MAN!*
NOW *THAT'S* WHAT I'M TALKING ABOUT...EXCEPT FOR THE DYING PART.

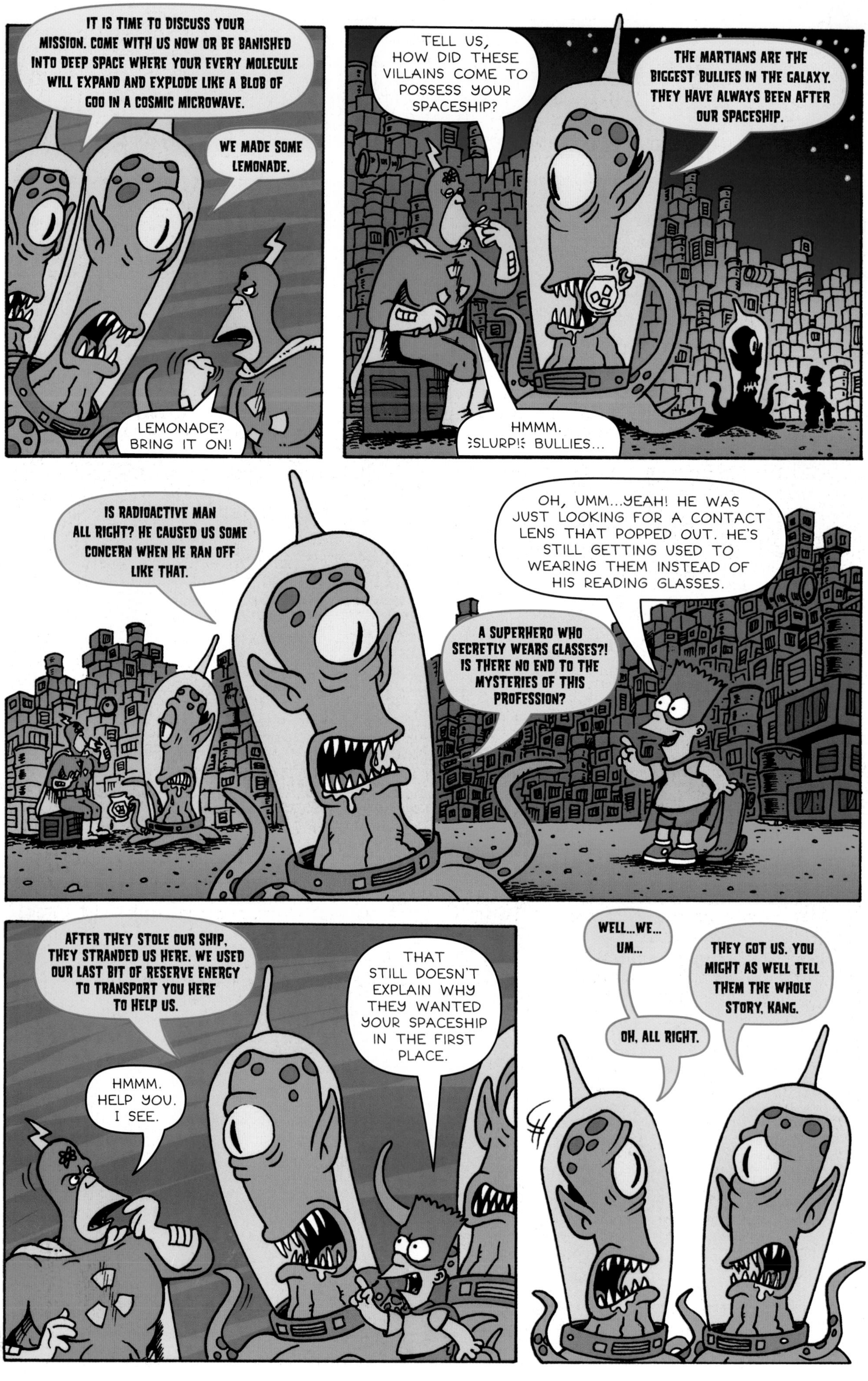
IT IS TIME TO DISCUSS YOUR MISSION. COME WITH US NOW OR BE BANISHED INTO DEEP SPACE WHERE YOUR EVERY MOLECULE WILL EXPAND AND EXPLODE LIKE A BLOB OF GOO IN A COSMIC MICROWAVE.
WE MADE SOME LEMONADE.
LEMONADE? BRING IT ON!
TELL US, HOW DID THESE VILLAINS COME TO POSSESS YOUR SPACESHIP?
THE MARTIANS ARE THE BIGGEST BULLIES IN THE GALAXY. THEY HAVE ALWAYS BEEN AFTER OUR SPACESHIP.
HMMM. SLURP! BULLIES...
IS RADIOACTIVE MAN ALL RIGHT? HE CAUSED US SOME CONCERN WHEN HE RAN OFF LIKE THAT.
OH, UMM...YEAH! HE WAS JUST LOOKING FOR A CONTACT LENS THAT POPPED OUT. HE'S STILL GETTING USED TO WEARING THEM INSTEAD OF HIS READING GLASSES.
A SUPERHERO WHO SECRETLY WEARS GLASSES?! IS THERE NO END TO THE MYSTERIES OF THIS PROFESSION?
AFTER THEY STOLE OUR SHIP, THEY STRANDED US HERE. WE USED OUR LAST BIT OF RESERVE ENERGY TO TRANSPORT YOU HERE TO HELP US.
HMMM. HELP YOU. I SEE.
THAT STILL DOESN'T EXPLAIN WHY THEY WANTED YOUR SPACESHIP IN THE FIRST PLACE.
WELL...WE... UM...
OH, ALL RIGHT.
THEY GOT US. YOU MIGHT AS WELL TELL THEM THE WHOLE STORY, KANG.

"WE HAD JUST RECEIVED A TOP SECRET MISSION FROM THE INTERGALACTIC COUNCIL."

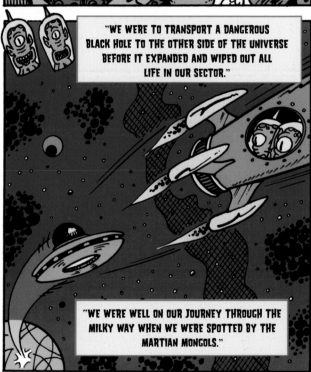

"WE WERE TO TRANSPORT A DANGEROUS BLACK HOLE TO THE OTHER SIDE OF THE UNIVERSE BEFORE IT EXPANDED AND WIPED OUT ALL LIFE IN OUR SECTOR."

"WE WERE WELL ON OUR JOURNEY THROUGH THE MILKY WAY WHEN WE WERE SPOTTED BY THE MARTIAN MONGOLS."

"WE WERE CAPTURED AND BROUGHT TO MARS. NOW THE MARTIANS HAVE THE BLACK HOLE AND OUR SPACESHIP."

WE NARROWLY ESCAPED THEIR GRASP. IF THEY OPEN THAT CONTAINER, WE'RE ALL DOOMED!

WHY DIDN'T YOU CONTACT THE INTERGALACTIC COUNCIL?

THEY WOULD HAVE FIRED US AND MADE FUN OF US BEHIND OUR BACKS.

WORRY NO LONGER. POINT US IN THE DIRECTION OF YOUR SHIP AND WE WILL DROP THE HAMMER OF JUSTICE UPON YOUR FOUL AND FIENDISH FOES!

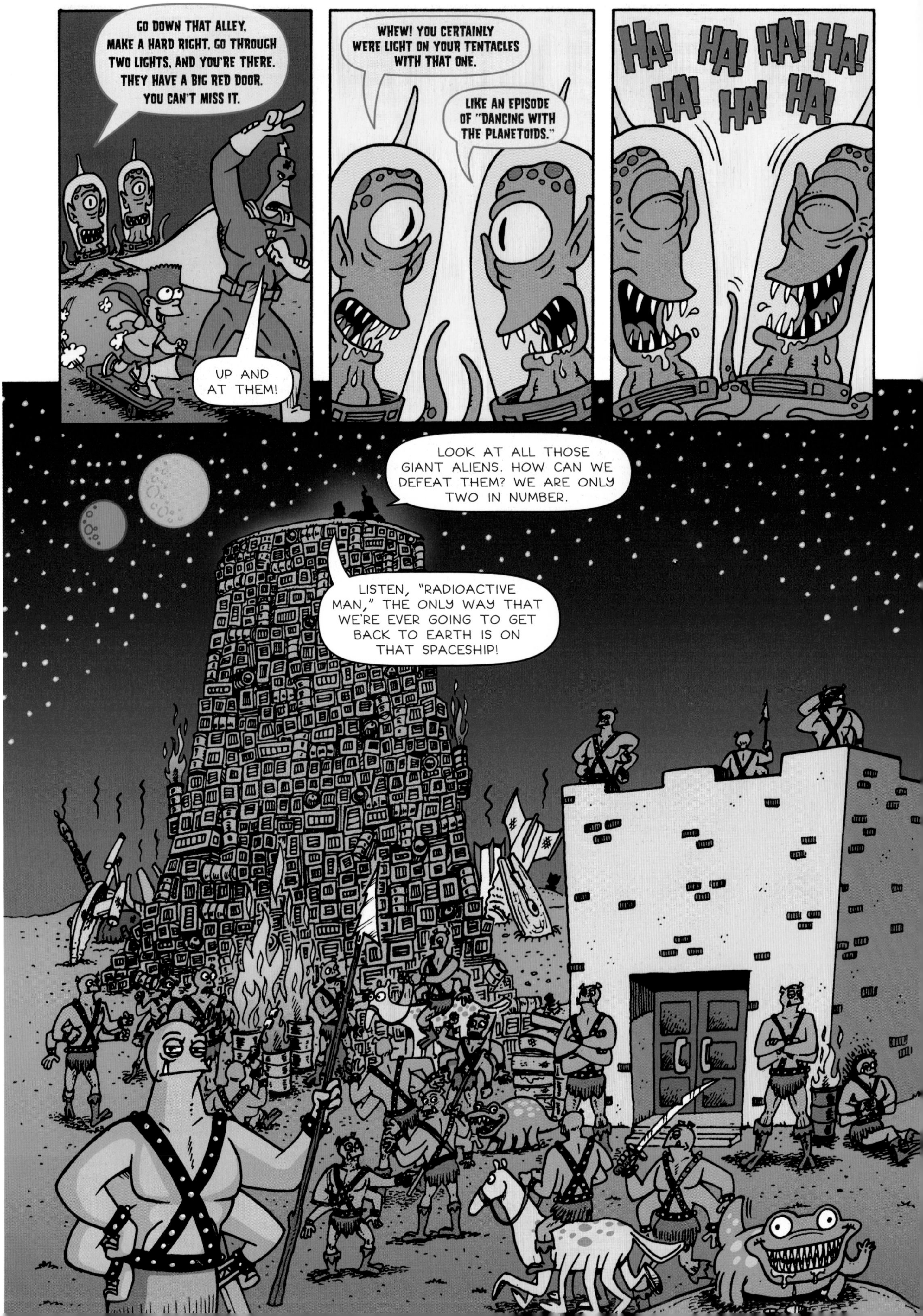

GO DOWN THAT ALLEY, MAKE A HARD RIGHT, GO THROUGH TWO LIGHTS, AND YOU'RE THERE. THEY HAVE A BIG RED DOOR. YOU CAN'T MISS IT.
UP AND AT THEM!
WHEW! YOU CERTAINLY WERE LIGHT ON YOUR TENTACLES WITH THAT ONE.
LIKE AN EPISODE OF "DANCING WITH THE PLANETOIDS."
HA! HA! HA! HA! HA! HA! HA!
LOOK AT ALL THOSE GIANT ALIENS. HOW CAN WE DEFEAT THEM? WE ARE ONLY TWO IN NUMBER.
LISTEN, "RADIOACTIVE MAN," THE ONLY WAY THAT WE'RE EVER GOING TO GET BACK TO EARTH IS ON THAT SPACESHIP!

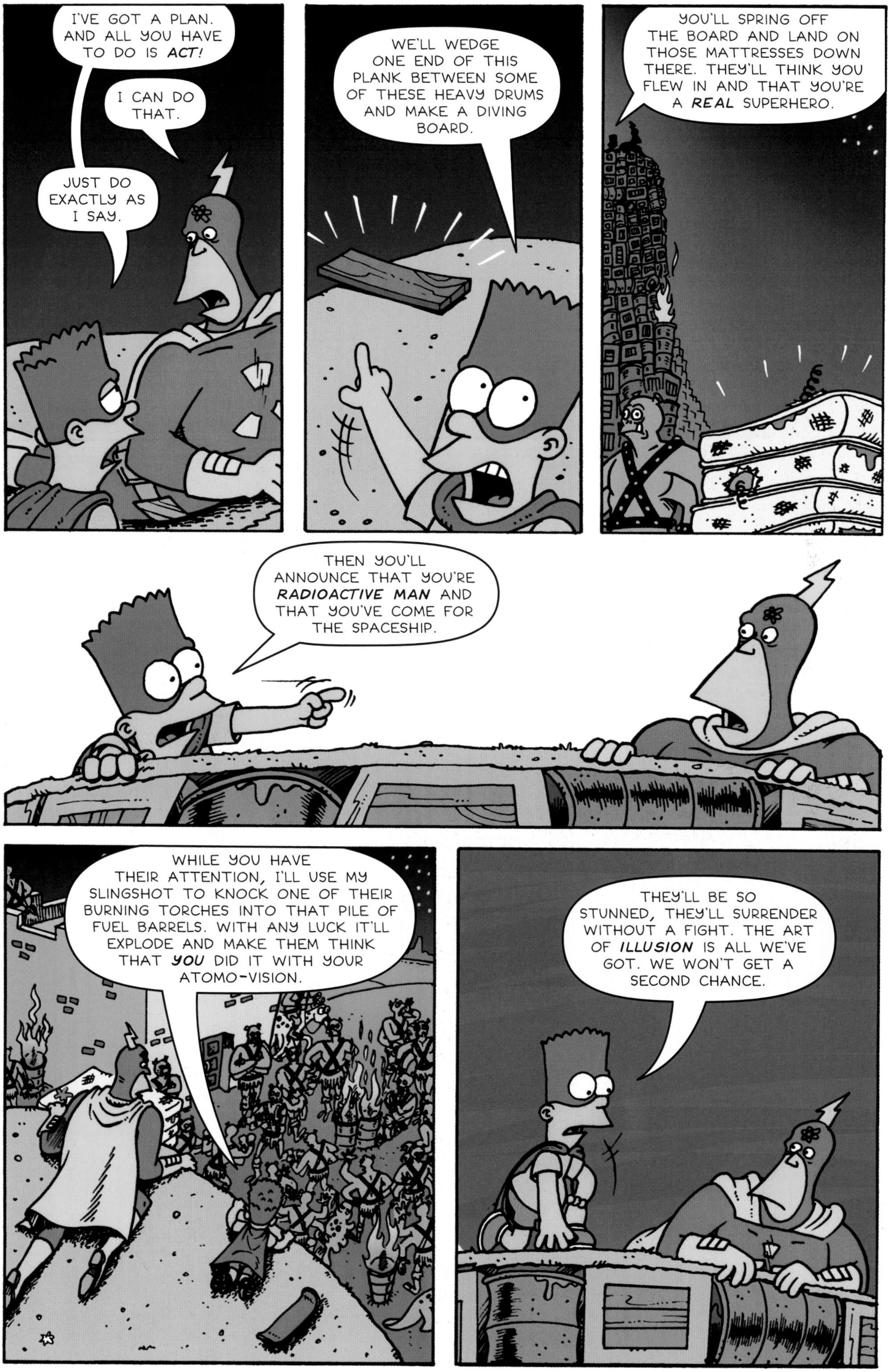

I'VE GOT A PLAN. AND ALL YOU HAVE TO DO IS ACT!
I CAN DO THAT.
JUST DO EXACTLY AS I SAY.
WE'LL WEDGE ONE END OF THIS PLANK BETWEEN SOME OF THESE HEAVY DRUMS AND MAKE A DIVING BOARD.
YOU'LL SPRING OFF THE BOARD AND LAND ON THOSE MATTRESSES DOWN THERE. THEY'LL THINK YOU FLEW IN AND THAT YOU'RE A REAL SUPERHERO.
THEN YOU'LL ANNOUNCE THAT YOU'RE RADIOACTIVE MAN AND THAT YOU'VE COME FOR THE SPACESHIP.
WHILE YOU HAVE THEIR ATTENTION, I'LL USE MY SLINGSHOT TO KNOCK ONE OF THEIR BURNING TORCHES INTO THAT PILE OF FUEL BARRELS. WITH ANY LUCK IT'LL EXPLODE AND MAKE THEM THINK THAT YOU DID IT WITH YOUR ATOMO-VISION.
THEY'LL BE SO STUNNED, THEY'LL SURRENDER WITHOUT A FIGHT. THE ART OF ILLUSION IS ALL WE'VE GOT. WE WON'T GET A SECOND CHANCE.

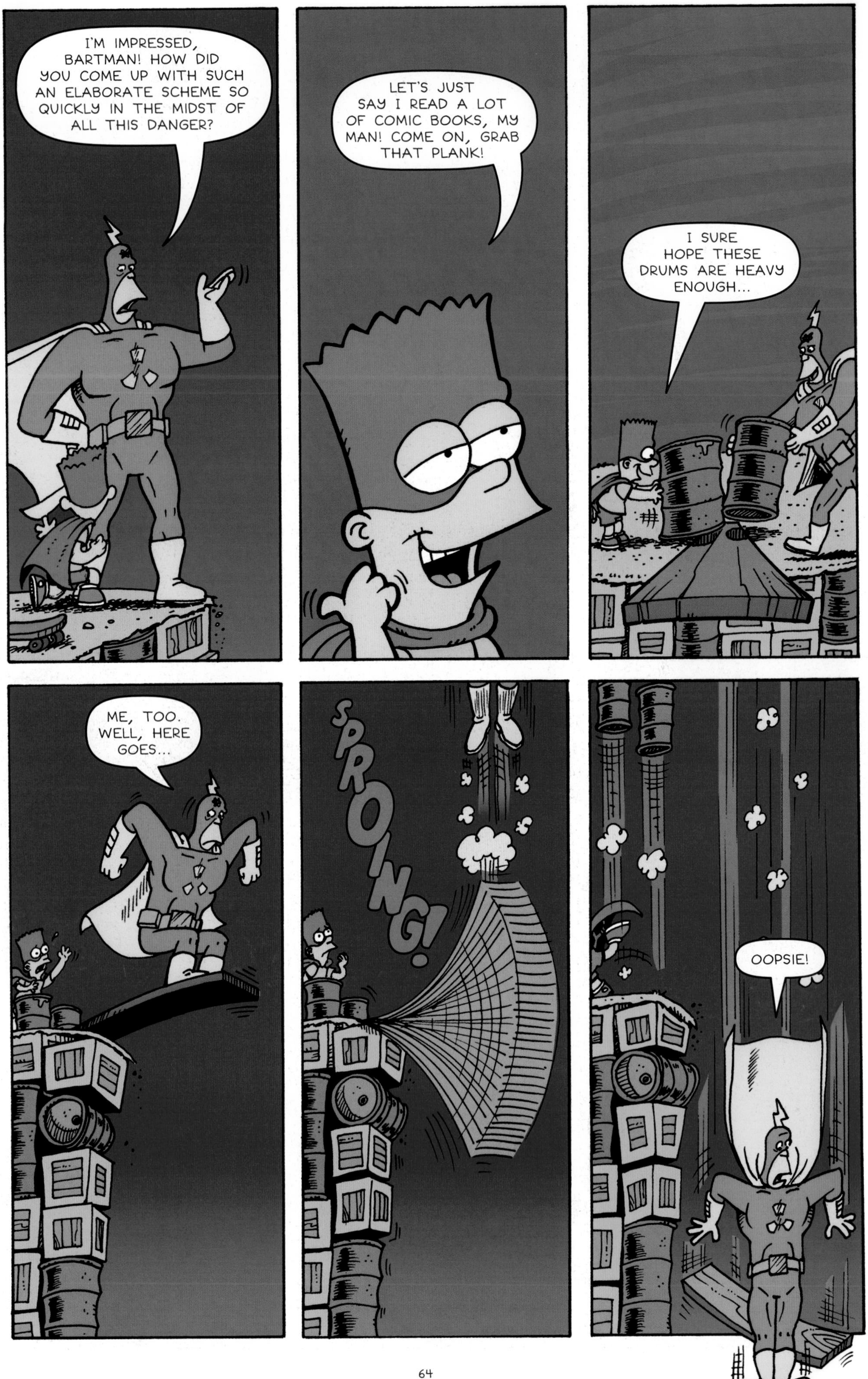
I'M IMPRESSED, BARTMAN! HOW DID YOU COME UP WITH SUCH AN ELABORATE SCHEME SO QUICKLY IN THE MIDST OF ALL THIS DANGER?
LET'S JUST SAY I READ A LOT OF COMIC BOOKS, MY MAN! COME ON, GRAB THAT PLANK!
I SURE HOPE THESE DRUMS ARE HEAVY ENOUGH...
ME, TOO. WELL, HERE GOES...
SPROING!
OOPSIE!

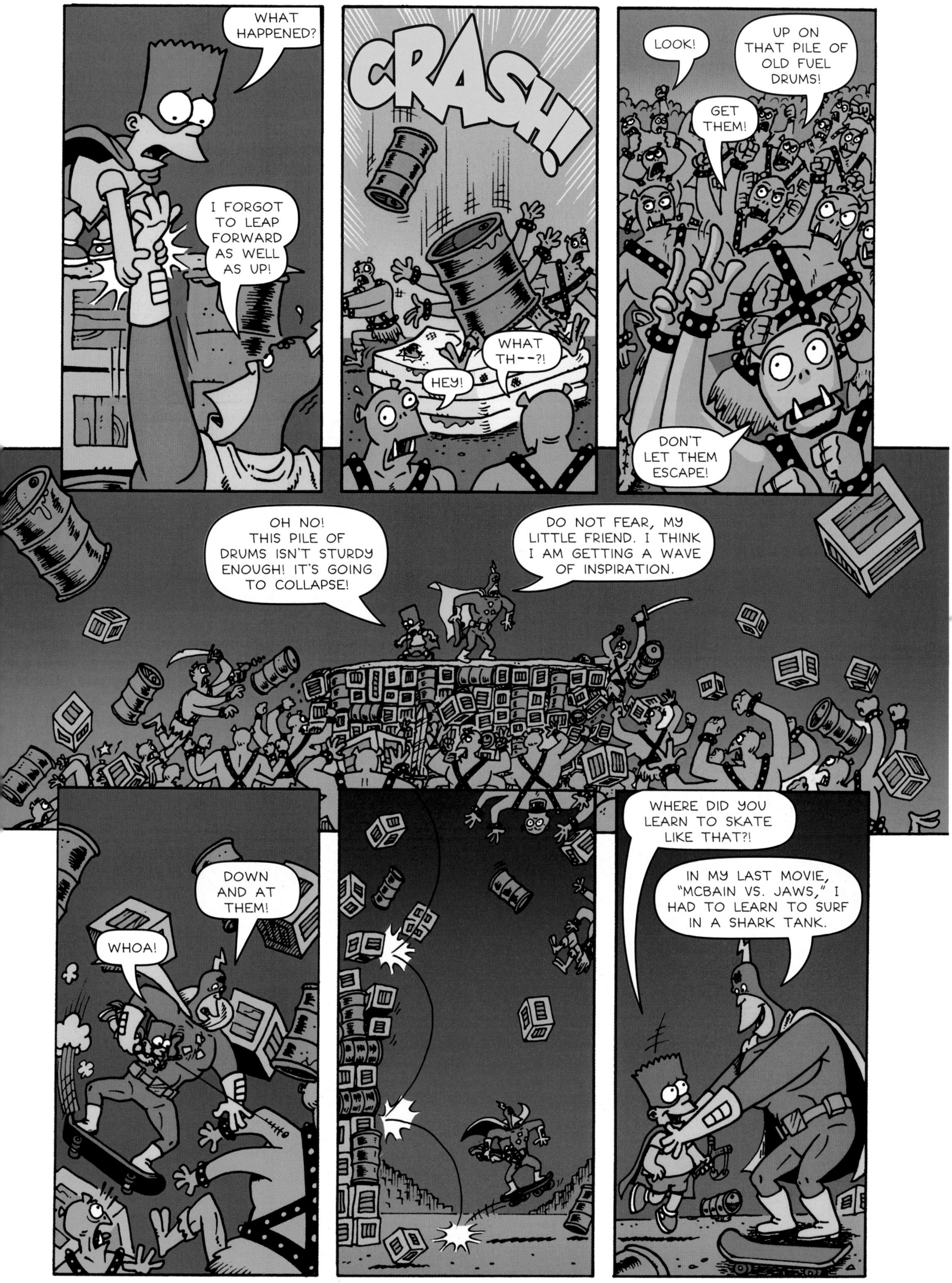
WHAT HAPPENED?
I FORGOT TO LEAP FORWARD AS WELL AS UP!
CRASH!
HEY!
WHAT TH--?!
LOOK!
UP ON THAT PILE OF OLD FUEL DRUMS!
GET THEM!
DON'T LET THEM ESCAPE!
OH NO! THIS PILE OF DRUMS ISN'T STURDY ENOUGH! IT'S GOING TO COLLAPSE!
DO NOT FEAR, MY LITTLE FRIEND. I THINK I AM GETTING A WAVE OF INSPIRATION.
WHOA!
DOWN AND AT THEM!
WHERE DID YOU LEARN TO SKATE LIKE THAT?!
IN MY LAST MOVIE, "MCBAIN VS. JAWS," I HAD TO LEARN TO SURF IN A SHARK TANK.

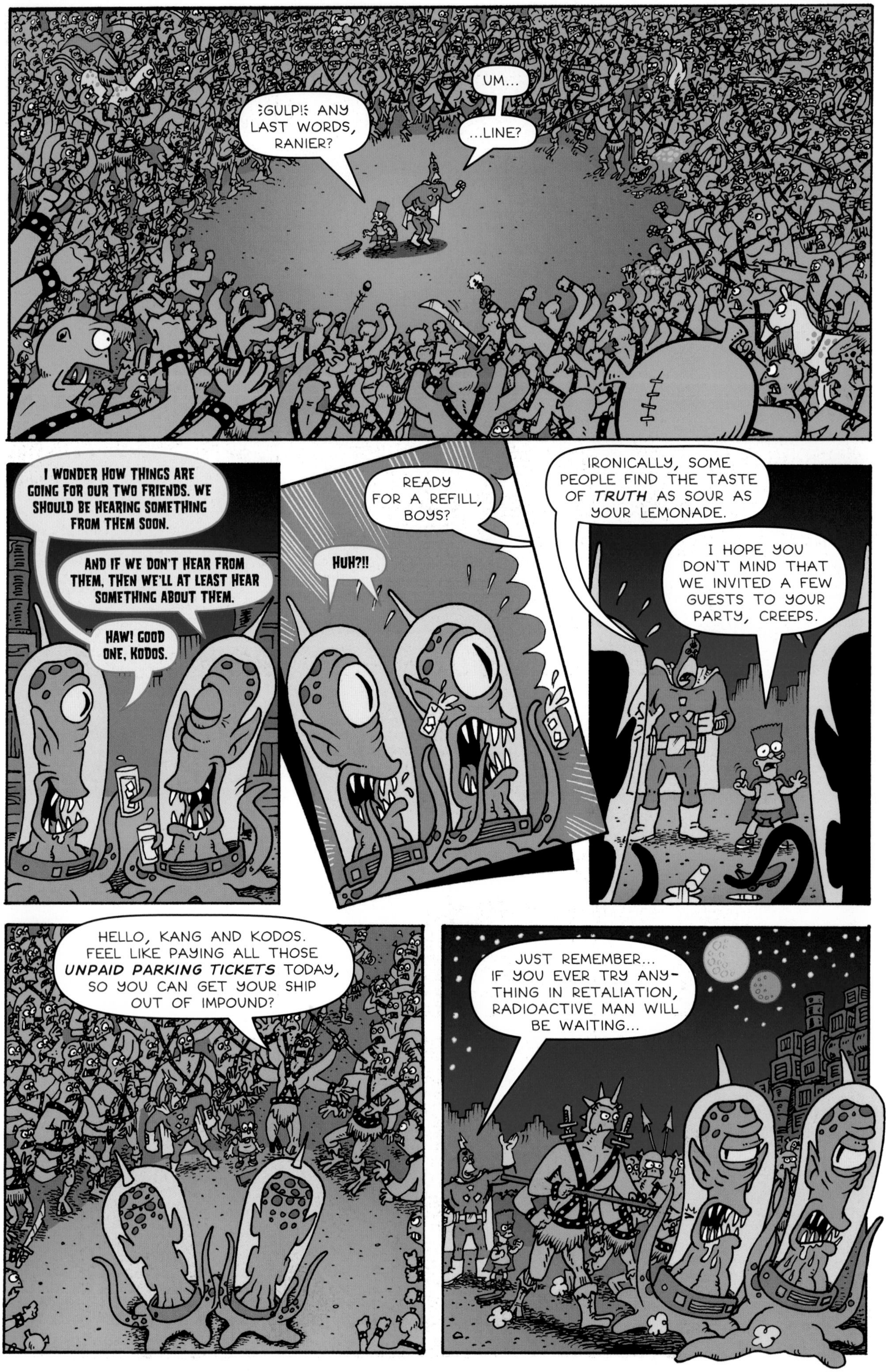

¡GULP!¡ ANY LAST WORDS, RANIER?
UM...
...LINE?
I WONDER HOW THINGS ARE GOING FOR OUR TWO FRIENDS. WE SHOULD BE HEARING SOMETHING FROM THEM SOON.
AND IF WE DON'T HEAR FROM THEM, THEN WE'LL AT LEAST HEAR SOMETHING ABOUT THEM.
HAW! GOOD ONE, KODOS.
READY FOR A REFILL, BOYS?
HUH?!!
IRONICALLY, SOME PEOPLE FIND THE TASTE OF TRUTH AS SOUR AS YOUR LEMONADE.
I HOPE YOU DON'T MIND THAT WE INVITED A FEW GUESTS TO YOUR PARTY, CREEPS.
HELLO, KANG AND KODOS. FEEL LIKE PAYING ALL THOSE UNPAID PARKING TICKETS TODAY, SO YOU CAN GET YOUR SHIP OUT OF IMPOUND?
JUST REMEMBER... IF YOU EVER TRY ANY-THING IN RETALIATION, RADIOACTIVE MAN WILL BE WAITING...

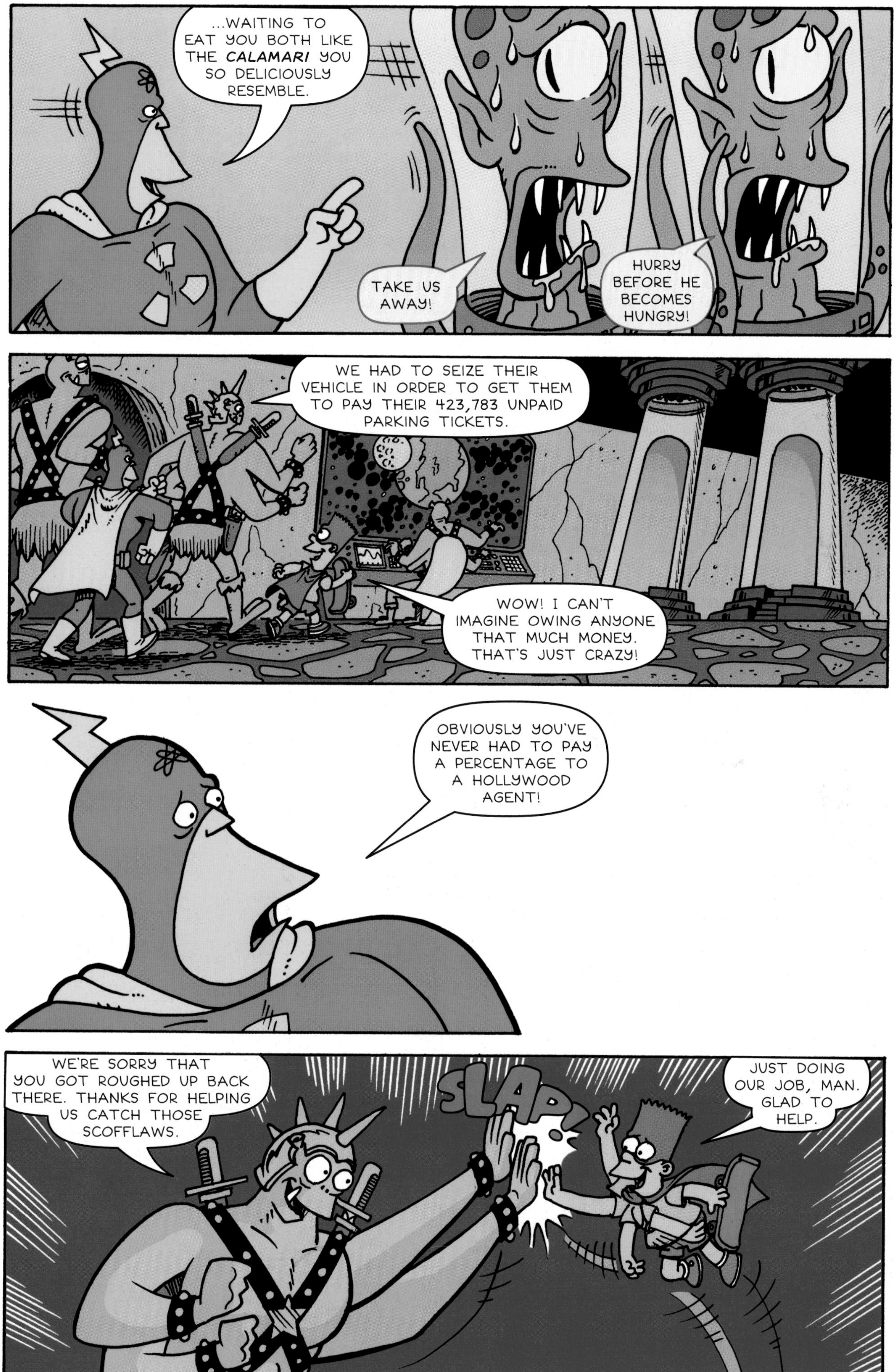
...WAITING TO EAT YOU BOTH LIKE THE **CALAMARI** YOU SO DELICIOUSLY RESEMBLE.
TAKE US AWAY!
HURRY BEFORE HE BECOMES HUNGRY!
WE HAD TO SEIZE THEIR VEHICLE IN ORDER TO GET THEM TO PAY THEIR 423,783 UNPAID PARKING TICKETS.
WOW! I CAN'T IMAGINE OWING ANYONE THAT MUCH MONEY. THAT'S JUST CRAZY!
OBVIOUSLY YOU'VE NEVER HAD TO PAY A PERCENTAGE TO A HOLLYWOOD AGENT!
WE'RE SORRY THAT YOU GOT ROUGHED UP BACK THERE. THANKS FOR HELPING US CATCH THOSE SCOFFLAWS.
SLAP!
JUST DOING OUR JOB, MAN. GLAD TO HELP.

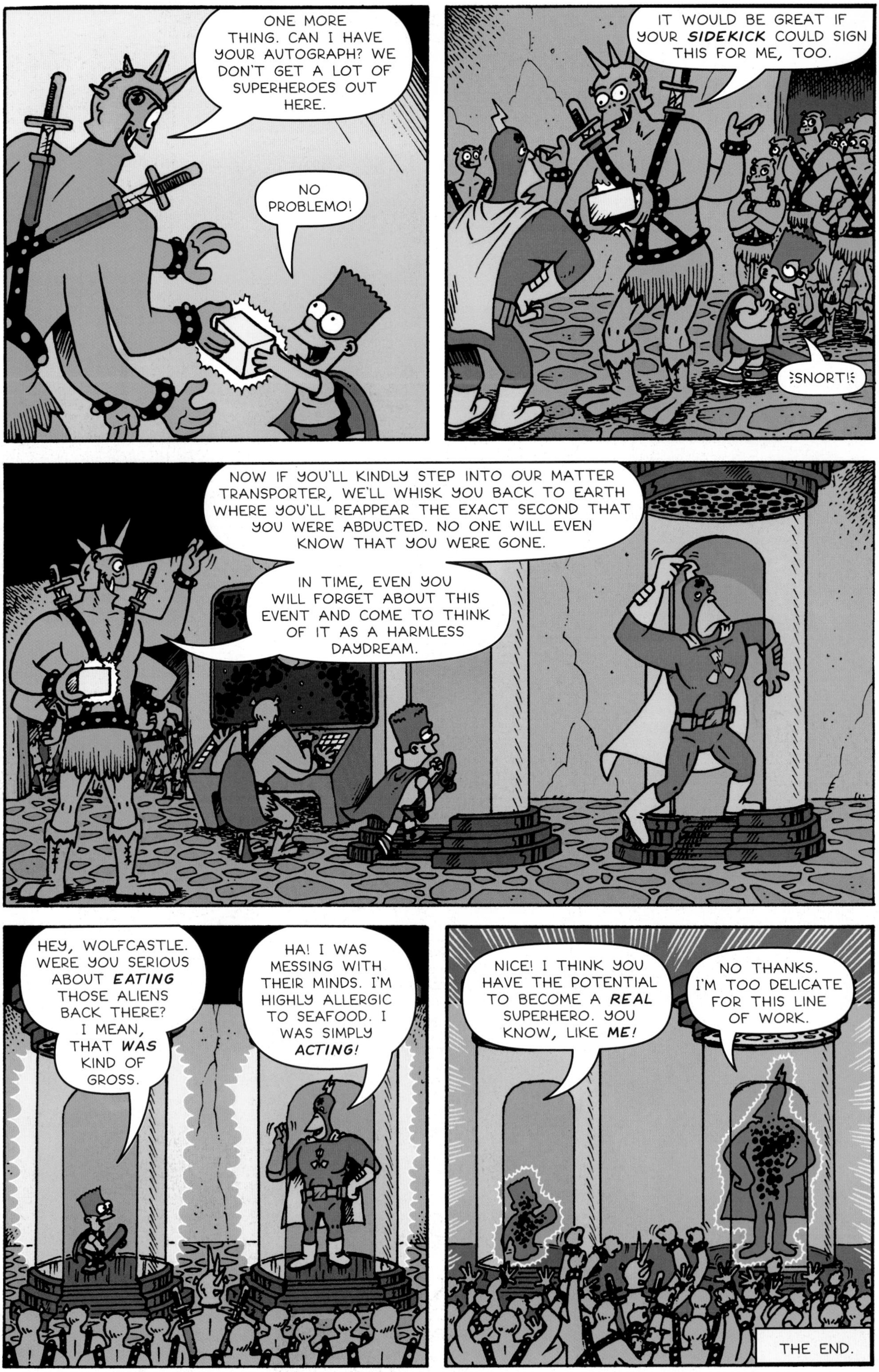
ONE MORE THING. CAN I HAVE YOUR AUTOGRAPH? WE DON'T GET A LOT OF SUPERHEROES OUT HERE.
NO PROBLEMO!
IT WOULD BE GREAT IF YOUR SIDEKICK COULD SIGN THIS FOR ME, TOO.
SNORT!
NOW IF YOU'LL KINDLY STEP INTO OUR MATTER TRANSPORTER, WE'LL WHISK YOU BACK TO EARTH WHERE YOU'LL REAPPEAR THE EXACT SECOND THAT YOU WERE ABDUCTED. NO ONE WILL EVEN KNOW THAT YOU WERE GONE.
IN TIME, EVEN YOU WILL FORGET ABOUT THIS EVENT AND COME TO THINK OF IT AS A HARMLESS DAYDREAM.
HEY, WOLFCASTLE. WERE YOU SERIOUS ABOUT EATING THOSE ALIENS BACK THERE? I MEAN, THAT WAS KIND OF GROSS.
HA! I WAS MESSING WITH THEIR MINDS. I'M HIGHLY ALLERGIC TO SEAFOOD. I WAS SIMPLY ACTING!
NICE! I THINK YOU HAVE THE POTENTIAL TO BECOME A REAL SUPERHERO. YOU KNOW, LIKE ME!
NO THANKS. I'M TOO DELICATE FOR THIS LINE OF WORK.
THE END.

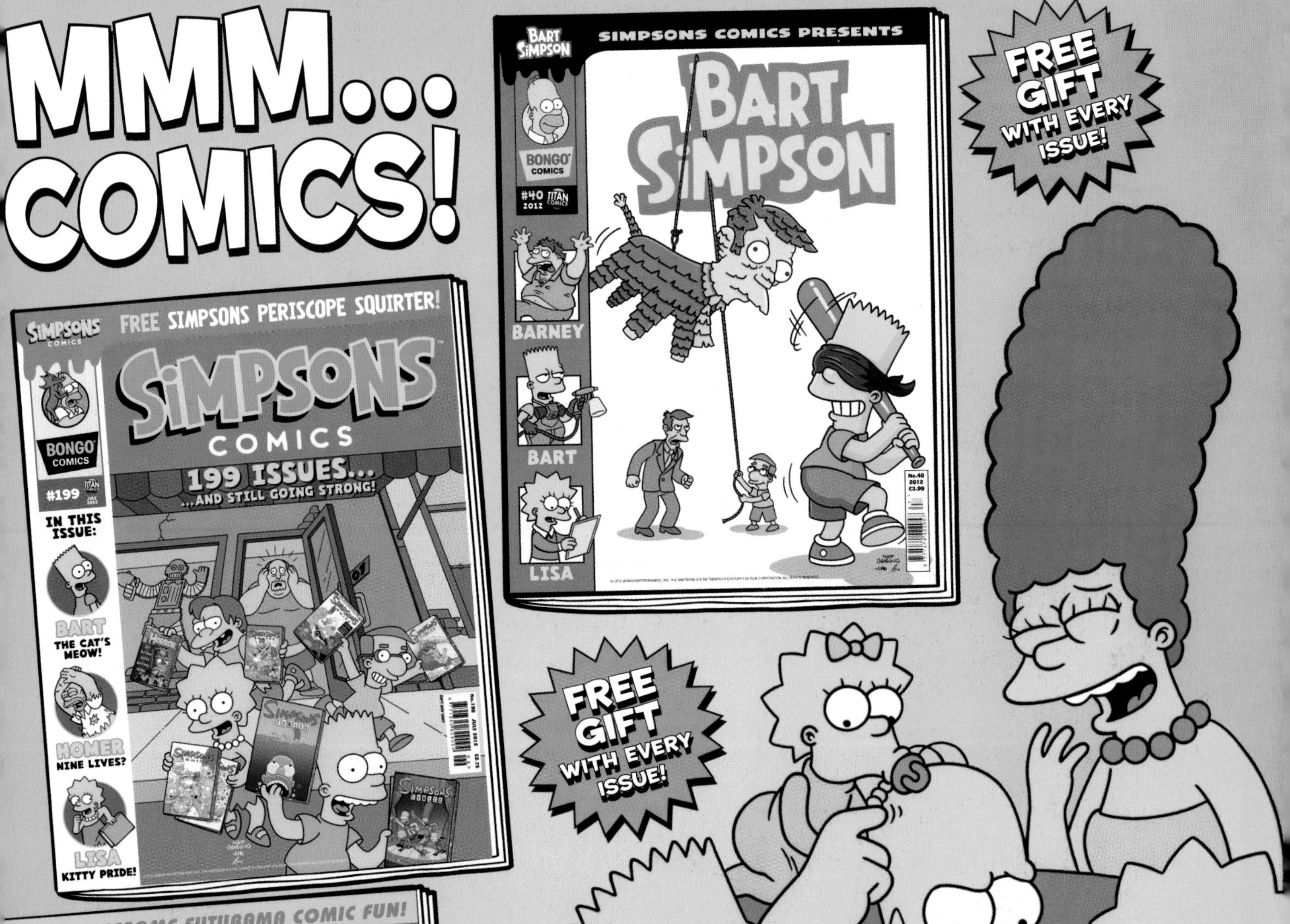
MMM... COMICS!
SIMPSONS COMICS PRESENTS
BART SIMPSON
BONGO COMICS
#40 2012
BARNEY
BART
LISA
FREE GIFT WITH EVERY ISSUE!
FREE SIMPSONS PERISCOPE SQUIRTER!
SIMPSONS COMICS
199 ISSUES... ...AND STILL GOING STRONG!
#199
IN THIS ISSUE:
BART THE CAT'S MEOW!
HOMER NINE LIVES?
LISA KITTY PRIDE!
FREE GIFT WITH EVERY ISSUE!
AWESOME FUTURAMA COMIC FUN!
FUTURAMA comics
#63 £3.25
BEWARE: ANGRY OWLS!
SUBSCRIBE TO SIMPSONS COMICS
MATT GROENING

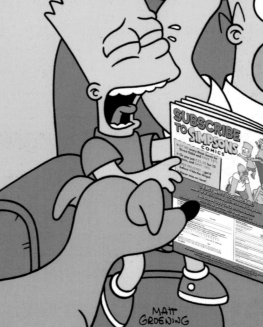

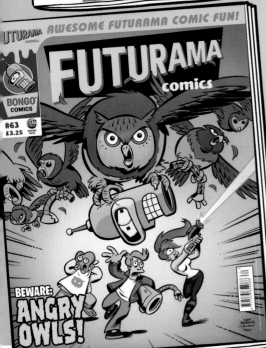

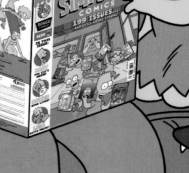